A key word in this powerful book is 'frontlines.' But here the life-and-death agonies are happening not in wartime. We now see a different time of darkness – what Camus had called La Peste. This is the gripping story of the human mind's inner struggle to transcend such darkness.

– Gregory Nagy, Harvard University

Freud asserted that 'no mortal can keep a secret', which, in turn, made '... the task of making conscious the most hidden recesses of the mind... quite possible to accomplish.' Unfortunately, few among us really know how to listen to others. Françoise Davoine's *Pandemics, Wars, Trauma and Literature: Echoes from the Front Lines* is a master class in listening to people individually and through their collective voice as expressed in history and literature in order to perceive deep truths which, once heard, inform effective response at every level of society.

– Harold Kudler, MD, Associate Consultant Professor, Department of Psychiatry and Behavioral Sciences, Duke University

In this beautiful book, we hear the voices of frontline healthcare workers in the COVID pandemic who speak to us from the region between life and death, where they accompany their ill and dying patients and bear witness to our current catastrophe from within its unthinkable center. The therapeutic innovations of these caretakers and their techniques of listening and of story-telling become the starting point for Davoine's remarkable history of the psychiatric and psychoanalytic encounters with trauma and madness— as they emerged from social upheaval, war and plague—and of a Western literary tradition that has served both as therapy and testimony to centuries of disaster. Framing her account with her personal journey—and that of her late husband and co-author Jean-Max Gaudilliére—in the psychoanalysis of madness, Davoine reveals, through her analyses of therapists, writers, philosophers, and cultural rituals, the joint 'transference' between patient and caretaker, sufferer and listener, as they guide each other through calamity and help pass on, to us, the histories most at risk of being lost.

– Cathy Caruth, Class of 1916 Professor of English at Cornell and Professor in both English and Comparative Literature

In this work we see how Françoise Davoine is a major force moving therapy of trauma into the mainstream of psychoanalysis. She does this by connecting the inner experience of the analyst, to that of the patient, and the personal history of both to the larger history of society. All the while weaving in the powerful record which writers such as Cervantes, Sterne, Boccaccio and others have given us of trauma in their own lives. She can do all this not only because she understands and respects the essence of the psychoanalytic process, but because she is fully open to all that literature and history teach us. She also understands the nature of the psychic wounds (the cut-out unconscious) caused by severe trauma.

While the mind may be shocked by severe trauma and catastrophe, left with a psychic black hole which absorbs endless amounts of the meaning and joy of life, perhaps transforming into madness, Davoine understands the cure analytic treatment and links with comprehending others who know how to collaborate in retrieving the cut-out parts, and fill the black hole with new structure for memory. She demonstrates in her very writing the particular kind of so-called free association essential to access the unrepressed unconscious.

For the work at hand, she had the presence of mind to juxtapose the experiences of five health care workers in the Covid pandemic, with Thomas Salmon's four principles of frontline psychiatry: Proximity, Immediacy, Expectancy and Simplicity. Which as it happens, comprise both the key to the workers' surviving the pandemic, and critical features of effective psychoanalysis:

Translated to the therapeutic context—
Proximity: ability of the analyst to take in qualities of the trauma;
Immediacy: allowing (right here and now) transference experiencing of the traumatic events;
Expectancy: expecting the patient to recover; and
Simplicity: seeing the historical links clearly.

– Arthur Blank Jr. MD, Faculty, Washington-Baltimore
Society for Psychoanalysis; Clinical Professor of Psychiatry,
George Washington School of Medicine; Former National
Director of the Vet Centers, U.S. Dept of Veterans Affairs

Pandemics, Wars, Traumas and Literature

This book presents unique insights into the experiences of frontline medical workers during the COVID-19 pandemic, psychoanalytic work with trauma and perspectives from literature.

Part One presents a set of six 'testimonies', transcribed from video interviews conducted by Françoise Davoine with nurses, doctors and intensive care anaesthesiologists. These interviews are drawn on in Part Two, 'Frontline Psychoanalysis', which tells the story of transference related to catastrophic events, discovered and subsequently abandoned by Freud when he gave up the psychoanalysis of trauma in 1897. Davoine discusses the occurrence of this specific type of transference, both during the First World War, in which psychotherapists modified classical techniques and invented the psychoanalysis of madness in order to treat traumatised soldiers, and during the current and previous pandemics. The book also considers social and artistic responses to trauma, from the popularity of the Theatre of Fools after the Black Death ravaged Europe, to the psychotherapy described in such circumstances by Boccaccio's *Decameron*.

This accessible work offers an insightful reflection on trauma and the human experience. *Pandemics, Wars, Traumas and Literature* will be of great interest to psychoanalysts in practice and in training, psychoanalytic psychotherapists and academics and scholars of literature.

Françoise Davoine is a psychoanalyst based in France. She is former Professor at the Centre for the Study of Social Movements, École des Hautes Études en Sciences Sociales (EHESS) in Paris, where she and Jean-Max Gaudillière conducted a weekly seminar on 'Madness and the Social Link'. She presents internationally and is the author of many books and articles.

Pandemics, Wars, Traumas and Literature

Echoes from the Front Lines

Françoise Davoine

TRANSLATED BY AGNÈS JACOB

Routledge
Taylor & Francis Group

LONDON AND NEW YORK

Cover image: Getty images

First published 2022
by Routledge
2 Park Square, Milton Park, Abingdon, Oxon OX14 4RN

and by Routledge
605 Third Avenue, New York, NY 10158

Routledge is an imprint of the Taylor & Francis Group, an informa business

© 2022 Françoise Davoine

British Library Cataloguing-in-Publication Data
A catalogue record for this book is available from the British Library

Library of Congress Cataloging-in-Publication Data
A catalog record has been requested for this book

ISBN: 978-1-032-19081-5 (hbk)
ISBN: 978-1-032-19083-9 (pbk)
ISBN: 978-1-003-25759-2 (ebk)

DOI: 10.4324/9781003257592

Typeset in Times New Roman
by codeMantra

Contents

Foreword

In December 2019, PUF editors, philosopher Frédéric Worms and sociologist Nathalie Zaccaï-Reyners, invited me to write about "Trauma, Health Care and Literature" for their book series "Questions de soins" (The Philosophy of Care).

In March, the pandemic was declared. The French President ordered a national lockdown, announcing a "state of war" in a speech filled with references to the Great War. Historian Stéphane Audoin-Rouzeau reacted to the speech by defining "wartime" as a time when the future is unpredictable and a return to life as it was before is impossible. Then came the deconfinement in May, while on near and distant fronts a second wave of the disease was expected.

In April, my son Brice Gaudillière, anaesthesiologist at the Stanford University Medical Center and head of an immunology laboratory, put me in touch with one of his French colleagues, Franck Verdonk, another intensive care anaesthesiologist and researcher, who had hastily returned to his hospital in Paris.

Thanks to him, I started to collect testimonies about frontline care: his testimony, those of Jessica and Lucie, who are also intensive care anaesthesiologists, and those of nurses Nanosy and Emmanuelle. Through my other son, Pierre, who was then the commander of the air base serving as a take-off point for aircraft equipped for the transfer of patients, I recorded the testimony of Anne Lise, emergency doctor with the Fire Brigade in Eastern Paris, who took part in evacuations. When the confinement ended in France, Jessica left to work on the front lines in her native Guyana, where the epidemic was raging.

These six video conference interviews reminded me of "frontline psychotherapy", devised during the Great War by psychiatrists and analysts working on the front lines in military hospitals in Europe and the United States. After the war, they became pioneers of the psychoanalysis of psychosis, looking at delusions as a means of finding one's bearings in extreme situations, which patients in an induced coma experience as well.

I will transcribe these testimonies as they were given to me, without commenting on them, since they speak for themselves. I will, however, connect them to the principles of this frontline approach, something I knew nothing about when I started working as an analyst at a public psychiatric hospital in the 1970s. At the time, mainstream psychoanalysis stayed away from psychosis, except in the field of child analysis, based on the presumption that "transference" was impossible without verbal communication. Yet I was discovering that the patients at the psychiatric hospital were acutely aware of our relationship, constantly testing my ability to "hold out" when psychic survival was at stake. "To 'hold out' is a term used during the Great War", Audoin-Rouzeau reminds us, in a situation one endures "without knowing how it will end, but hoping it will be soon". This perseverance, which can be taken for obstinacy, relies on a certain experience with a different temporality, cut off from the past, and having no foreseeable end.

This book will be composed of two parts. The first, entitled "Testimonies", consists of the transcription of the words of frontline healthcare professionals, who speak to intubated patients on the threshold of the temporal chasm in which they seem to disappear. When these witnesses speak of "transference", it is to refer to interactions with the patient's current state in the course of their professional practice. Their testimony, when I heard it, resonated with the principles of "frontline psychotherapy", discovered by therapists drafted to work on the front lines of recent wars. I will present their findings as a way of providing a framework for the six testimonies gathered on the front lines of the pandemic, thanks to Franck Verdonk, to whom I am greatly indebted.

The second part of the book, entitled "Frontline Psychoanalysis", will tell the story of this transference related to catastrophic events, only to be abandoned afterwards. It all started with Freud's decision to give up the psychoanalysis of trauma, in September 1897, although he returned to it several times: through the analysis of literary works, and again after the outbreak of the First World War. I will discuss the discovery of this specific type of transference, first in wartime and then during the pandemic, and describe how therapists treating the traumatised soldiers of the Great War were forced to modify classical analytic techniques and to invent the psychoanalysis of psychosis after the war.

I will also be using literary references, just as we did in the weekly seminar "Madness and the Social Link" that Jean-Max Gaudillière and I conducted together at the EHESS in Paris for 40 years, until his death in 2015.[1] Based on our experience as psychoanalysts in psychiatric hospitals, in the seminars we engaged in dialogue with authors who linked the madness of their characters to historical catastrophes.

In the Middle Ages, it was believed that "Madness is more intelligence (from the Latin *ingenium*) than fate".[2] Indeed, when Folly speaks in Erasmus'

The Praise of Folly,[3] she asserts her intelligence: "Who can set me out better than myself?" And she concludes her speech by saying: "'Tis Folly, and a woman, that has spoken".

This feminine agency personified by Mother Folly in the *Sotties* of the 15th century[4]—a Theatre of Fools, very popular after the Great Plague and the Hundred Years' War—takes over when the law of men collapses. She embodies hope in frontline psychotherapy, whose aim is to inscribe into the past an unforgettable memory which haunts the present. I believe she is as old as wars and pandemics, as I am told by Boccaccio's *Decameron*,[5] which I read during the first lockdown. Written just after the peak of the plague epidemic in Florence in 1348, the book describes a psychotherapy enacted while escaping the zone of death in the city. Seven young women convince three young men to go with them to the country, where the therapy consists of telling ten stories a day for ten days. The six testimonies which follow echo these stories from across the centuries.

Notes

1 Gaudillière, J.-M., *Madness and the Social Link* (Seminars 1985–2000); *The Birth of a Political Self* (Seminars 2001–2014), London: Routledge, 2020.
2 De Rotelande, H. (late 12th century), *Ipomedon*, Paris: Klincksieck, 1979.
3 Erasmus, D., *The Praise of Folly*, Aeterna Press, 2010.
4 Davoine, F., *Mother Folly*, Stanford, CA: Stanford University Press, 2014.
5 Boccaccio, G., *The Decameron*, London: Penguin Classics, 2003.

Acknowledgements

My profound thanks go to Frédéric Worms and Nathalie Zaccai Reyners, who had the idea for this book, whose meanders Nathalie followed closely until its publication. It took an unexpected turn when the pandemic broke out. Brice Gaudillière, anaesthesiologist and researcher at Stanford, put me in contact with his colleague Franck Verdonk, who had hastily come back to Paris. Without Franck, the testimonies given by Jessica, Lucie, Emmanuelle, Nanosy and Anne-Lise about their work on the front lines of emergency medicine and Intensive Care would not have been recorded. I thank them for the trust they granted me during our exchanges. This book took shape by connecting their testimonies with First World War forward psychotherapy, thanks to valuable advice from historian Stéphane Audoin-Rouzeau. I am very grateful for his constructive suggestions and his reassurance. I am also grateful for the invaluable critical reading provided by Pierre and Sophie Gaudillière.

Part I

Testimonies

May 7, 2020: Lucie, Jessica, Franck

- Proximity: fear and joy

— Jessica: In the beginning, when the crisis started, we realised what our role as medical doctors in society really meant. Until then we didn't necessarily feel it ourselves. Despite the fear, because I must admit that I was very frightened. Not only for my own health but also for that of my partner and my family; I was afraid of being exposed to the virus, but despite the fear I really wanted to be involved in the overall fight.

I must admit, I tend to have a saviour complex, and I wanted to save as many people as possible. I was especially close to some patients, I still remember their names and their faces, particularly three of them. I lost one and I was very upset when it happened; later, I could express what I felt. We were able to save the two others and I still think of them. Now I have to let go, but we talk about them.

— Lucie: If I may add this to what Jessica said, there is something striking with Covid as far as I am concerned, and the others too, I believe: the joy of getting patients out of a critical state. We are always happy when one of our patients comes out of Intensive Care, but it depends on the condition involved. Sometimes we have doubts, like when the person is undernourished. I am not always satisfied, results can be mixed.

But with Covid, since our patients were younger, since they had no major comorbidities to start with, I have the impression that we had more joy, much more than usual. We were not all working on the same floor, but as soon as a patient left the Intensive Care Unit, we told each other the news: Mister So and So came out, Mrs. Such and Such is doing well—and this is something that doesn't always happen; there was a lot of joy.

DOI: 10.4324/9781003257592-1

- ## Hope

— Jessica: Although the three patients I talked about were special, we do everything we can for each of them. When they are in a coma, I try to talk to them, I don't know if it's a good thing. I tell them: "You're going to get well".

— Françoise: Even when you don't know what the outcome will be?

— All respondents: Often. We don't know that for most of them.

— Françoise: When do you notice that they have taken a turn for the better?

— Lucie: It's very hard to tell, it's not until much later. In fact, when they improve, it's very sudden, and we can take them off the ventilator in two or three days. But these patients have had a long course of illness, they have been hospitalised for over a month. All of a sudden, something changes and they are better. In truth, it's impossible to predict when they will suddenly improve.

- ## Fear before the battle

— Jessica: Many seriously ill patients arrived all at the same time.

— Lucie: It happened all of a sudden. We were using 150% of our critical care capacity. Luckily, many doctors arrived as backup. During our shifts we were treating 16 patients, after we had treated only 4 during the day shift just before, as usual.

— Jessica: The hardest part was when we were waiting for them. We started to free up beds and move them around. We heard what was happening outside, through the media, in Eastern France where it was like a flood, the hospitals were overwhelmed, like in Italy. I was afraid, I confess. You know, in this waiting period, when you have time to think, you prepare yourself like for a war—it was really like that.

I dreaded what might happen, I was afraid we would be overwhelmed, and that many people would die and I would take it very hard; even if we are doctors, we still have feelings.

— Lucie: The common feeling during the crisis is fear. Perhaps not for everyone at the same time. It made me cry before it actually started. And then, all at once, like a good little soldier, I stepped up to the task. I had just been appointed Chief of Anaesthesiology; I had had my position for four months. I was thinking—a pandemic to start my career, I'm not equipped for that, I won't be able to do it. I was afraid for my family and for myself. A quarter of our staff was infected by the virus.

- ## Urgency of action and nightmares

— Lucie: After a week, I was no longer afraid for my health or that of my family. When we started out, we knew very little. What we had heard, above all, was that the 30-year-old Chinese doctor who sounded the alarm had died. We didn't know that healthy people could transmit the virus. Still, it was a crucial moment, it was for this that I had studied medicine, now was the time.

— Jessica: I was very afraid that many young people would die and that we would have to tell their families, who could not be with them. I was afraid of being overwhelmed, that there would be a very bad atmosphere in our personal and professional lives. But that didn't happen, quite the contrary.

The first week, during my shifts, it was impossible to sleep, even if I wanted to. I had nightmares. I was evacuating the stress. In my dreams I saw the patients, and my family. Several times I even dreamed that I was the one who was sick and intubated. During the crisis I didn't feel afraid, but in my dreams I saw myself on a ventilator. It was very strange. I had the impression it was real, tangible. I would wake up in the middle of the shift and go back to the ward.

You know, all of us who are doctors are able to switch from fear to an operational mode, to forget, and to forget ourselves. For me, it happens in dreams. Fortunately we have them. We told ourselves that it was our role, no question about that. Not one single person said they would not do it. No one said: "I'll let someone else do it". It's a vocation.

• Transference

— Jessica: There was the young woman, 34 years old, that I became attached to because she was my age, my colour, she comes from an island and I come from Guyana. It was probably transference. Her mother was the same age as mine and had the same voice. Her condition was very serious and I was taking it very hard. I told her mother that I would do everything medically possible. One day, I found myself brushing her hair, helping with her grooming routine—which is something doctors never do. With this young woman, I was more hopeful than usual for such a serious case.

It's a funny story, everyone laughed at me. This woman had beautiful frizzy hair. The nurse and the nurse's aid had been unable to untangle it for three weeks. She had a huge knotted pile on top of her head, in which there was food and vomit. We spent two and a half hours washing and untangling her hair. I didn't want to cut off her beautiful hair. Her hair means a lot to a woman. I brought special products from home; I know them since I use them myself. We played hairdresser on one of my shifts. I made her two braids. She came out beautiful, magnificent. They took a picture of the doctor styling her patient's hair. I was happy doing it, I had time, and it brought us closer—the nurse, the nurse's aid and I. The three of us did it together. She was getting better. When she left, she was beautiful. It was satisfying for everyone to see our pretty patient leave.

- ## The breath on the phone

— Lucie: We are the ones who call the family, and it's unusual, since they can't be here. Usually, families are allowed to visit people in Intensive Care 24 hours a day, whenever they wish. But now it was impossible. Most of the time the contact by phone with families went very well, which is not always the case in critical care when patients have complicated conditions. Still, people understood, thanks to the extensive media coverage.

But it was difficult. We called them every day in the afternoon. They were waiting for our call, we only called once, and they answered right away. Often, we had nothing much to say: "He or she is stable". He or she is still alive. A sliver of life, and we heard a sigh, especially the first week. We heard a sigh of relief on the phone: alright, he or she is still with us.

— Jessica: There was this 52-year-old woman, with no pre-existing conditions. She was one of the least serious cases, and we lost her after two weeks. I was working during that period and I took care of her for 15 days. Her condition worsened overnight, and she died, leaving four children between 16 and 19. I was talking to her son on the phone, telling him she was stable, until she got so bad that we had to put her on a heart-lung machine. I gave her son hourly updates, I didn't know what would happen.

It was hard. I had to take care of the patient, that was my job, but also of her kids, I had to remember that they were children. When she died, we couldn't prevent it, we couldn't save her, and I called them.[1] I noticed that during this crisis people became a little more religious and held on to spirituality.

When I called them, they said they would pray for us, for the team and for their mother. They were waiting for my call. The phone only rang once. I gave the bad news to the son and the oldest daughter. Since they had not seen their mother, I said they could come to say good-bye to her. It was very important for them. I sent the exemption letter quickly, they didn't live far. All four of them came, I dressed them in protective clothing and they were able to say good-bye to their mother. I think they were the most touched by this, and by the daily phone calls.

- ## Simplicity, talking with families

— Lucie: Our contact with the families was very good. We didn't do it for this reason, but we have never been thanked so much. When we called them every day, they always said: "Thank-you, we're thinking of you" before hanging up. Usually, this never happens. I think they understood that we were also in distress. Like in this situation I never forgot:

When we were in the thick of it, patients had to be flown out to the West of France, because there was no more room in our hospital. Each day, we had to choose a stable patient who would be transported by helicopter. The patient I'm talking about, I didn't know where he was going, and the SAMU (Urgent Medical Aid Service) couldn't tell me. So I had to call the family and tell them that their loved one was taken somewhere, and I didn't know where or when. It was the hardest call I've had to make as an Intensive Care physician.

I think the family sensed my distress. The patient developed a complication during the flight and died very shortly after they landed. I still think of him. I don't know if without this trip he would still be alive. The family was very nice, despite everything—it can seem naïve to say "very nice"—but they were: "We know it's not your fault, we know you did everything you could". Still, their father was dead and I could not tell them where.

- **Patients in a coma hear what is said**

— Jessica: The patient I talked about, the youngest on the ward, was in such serious condition that a week before it was suggested she should be put on a heart-lung machine. We all thought she could die. But we held on to the idea that we didn't know this disease, that the patient was young, and that we would do everything possible, continue to treat her no matter what, go the extra mile, since other patients suddenly got better. This worked for most of our patients. Many of those we thought we would lose suddenly improved.

Then patients started to be transferred. We didn't take it well. It was frustrating to work with them and then not be there when they awoke, to see the results of our work. The 34-year-old woman was the first to be extubated; we were all there around her bed. She was completely lost, she was very scared, she didn't know who we were, but she recognised our voices because she had heard them during her coma. She was saying that we weren't listening to her, although we were all there in her room.

— Lucie: There's something else, aside from what I talked about before. We record the vital sign numbers for patients who arrive in a coma. One of my interns called these patients the P/F ratios, the respiratory ratio we calculate each day. On our four floors, all the patients are the same, with the same history, the same condition, they were all alike, for her, they were the P/F ratios.

— Jessica: Most patients found their bearings. They were quite coherent when we went into their rooms, but as soon as we left they started to cry. One young man cried all the time. When I was with him he talked about his wife and children; I arranged for him to talk to his mother on the phone. Afterwards, he started to cry, perhaps he realised that something terrible had happened to him. Suddenly, he was no longer himself. He alternated between anxiety and presence.

- **The home front**

— Lucie: I am incredibly lucky to have a family that supports me. My grandmother is 90. She has been through the war. I was worried about her because she was at risk. But in fact, compared to my parents and my aunts and uncles, she is very organised, has supplies neatly put away. She is very calm, very disciplined, she listens carefully to what I tell her. It's an unusual time. Fortunately. You learn a lot about yourself. I am happy, since there were times when you had to be there, and I was. Maybe not perfectly. Like a fireman who goes into the flames to rescue a baby on the third floor. You don't know what you're capable of doing until you have to do it.
— Jessica: My landlord put flowerpots on the staircase going to my apartment on the first floor.
— Lucie: Small tokens of appreciation are very important.

- **Plural body**

— Franck: I didn't go through what Lucie and Jess experienced since I was not there in the beginning. I didn't live through the horrible period of waiting. I arrived on the first of April, everything had already started. I was in a particular position because I was not part of a specific team. I was there to help. I went from one ward to another. I didn't have time to create bonds with patients or families. What I was most aware of was the human dynamics, something like the sense of a vocation.

  I saw something I had rarely seen before, a situation where everyone worked together towards the same goal, in a shared and positive dynamic. And everyone really set aside his own fears. The ones who became ill returned to work as soon as possible. Being quarantined was hard for them.

  Even the surgeons, who always complain about the shortage of anaesthesiologists or about something else, all contributed to the common task. Most of them put their efforts into things they were not used to doing, that they could have considered demeaning for their level of training. Some of them even became patient care assistants, working side by side with the medical and nursing staff. This collective dynamic was very beautiful, I would like it to continue.
— Lucie: I am happy I had this experience, which I hope will never present itself again. I am proud of us, that no one gave up and said I leave it to someone else. It's wonderful to see, a team like that.

— Jessica: I work in two wards, Anaesthesiology and shifts in Intensive Care. Usually, there is a distance between their staff, the doctors don't know each other. Now, we built closer relations by caring for patients together. And I hope we won't lose these relations, now that we've experienced what they're like. We had no problem assigning shifts. Everything went smoothly. In two months, there was not a single conflict.

• Good food

— Franck: We have to stay realistic. But I would really like this dynamic to continue, based on a desire to help the population. It was powerful, I found it beautiful. I don't know if we will be able to do it again. It's always in difficult times that we all help each other. Although in critical care we work more closely together, the crisis erased status differences even more.

Now that we have passed the peak, we will go back to our routines. We have never been so well fed, and that counts. Neighbours brought us gifts of food, the big food stores gave us quality products. Now we will go back to normal life, the support of the population will stop, and we'll be dealing with our accumulated fatigue; the hardest part is yet to come.

It's the opposite of a war. In a war, you sink into something hellish and you come out of it to resume normal life. But for us, it is now that we might hit a low point. Our fight was a good fight.

— Lucie: There is talk of giving health care professionals a raise. Today at lunch we had our last improved meal. Frankly, I would prefer not to have a raise, but to have better meals, especially during 24-hour shifts. I think they don't realise. When you've just come in at midnight and you get a platter of eggs, spinach and cheap pudding, at that hour of the night it can be depressing—a platter at one euro fifty per doctor.

• Negative discourses, far from experience

— Jessica: The public understands our work better, and appreciates what we do. At first, we were very happy to hear everyone clap at eight o'clock. It made me cry, because I was working at the hospital the whole day then. I hope we will hold on to this attitude, because in France—I don't know how it is in other countries doctors are often seen as the bad guys. Now it was the opposite.

— Lucie: In the media, they focused only on the negative. I used to tell my partner that I didn't recognise myself in what they were saying. It was all about bad management. I found that really sad, since we were not managing so badly, and we had saved many people. My impression of our work in the field was that it was much more positive, while around us they talked only of catastrophe. From my humble perspective, I think we managed quite well. It got very crowded, we were not working as usual, but everything did not fall apart. We succeeded.

— Jessica: People have a great propensity for looking at the bad side. The same people who didn't want the lockdown are now against ending the lockdown.

May 22, 2020. Testimony of Anne Lise, emergency doctor with the fire brigade in Eastern Paris

• I go to people's homes

It's strange to applaud, but it's a sign of gratitude that you have to accept for what it is.

My experience is different from that of the hospital staff. I work outside the hospital, I go to people's homes. At first, we didn't understand that it would be a pandemic. And I was not the only one. We thought that things would settle down, like a flu outbreak, and that there would be no problem. But it just got worse. At first, we hardly wore any protection, but as things progressed we dressed up like astronauts.

In the beginning, our work was very hard. We had a lot of cases, we didn't know much about the infection, we didn't really know what to do. We were called to the homes of patients whose vital signs were bad but whose clinical symptoms were not too serious. It was very strange. Plus, working with all that protective gear on is very disconcerting and exhausting. It was hard to orient ourselves in the situation, so that communicating with the patients became difficult. They could not see our faces. When we work in prehospital emergency care, we see the patient in a critical state. Even dressed normally, it's hard to communicate since the patient is in shock, but in this situation it was extremely difficult.

We had many cardiac arrests that were not counted, people over 70 mostly, whom we could not resuscitate. Dealing with the family is complicated, because the death is sudden and unexpected.

• Absence of funeral rites

I work in the East of Paris, the 18th, 19th, 20th *arrondissements*, and the 93 banlieue, where the population is very mixed. For North Africans, who usually send the bodies home for burial, there was shock and disbelief, because bodies could not be flown to the homeland during the pandemic.

Honestly, we were not prepared for this. The hardest thing for me was not announcing someone's death, which is part of our work, even when death is unexpected. But now, we were placing the dead in body bags—you can imagine how impersonal it is! We tell the family there will be no personal care of the body, nothing, since it's forbidden during the epidemic. After they are in the body bag, the family must not touch them. It's awful. They never see them again, never, not even in a coffin for burial. Because death is so sudden, many family members are not there, and they will never see the face of their loved one again. This was the most difficult thing for me, the most inhuman. It was rarely mentioned.

When we announce the death, they are always flabbergasted, they never expected it. I try to explain about the Coronavirus epidemic, that it's everywhere, that it's spreading and this is why the government established rules to protect those who are in contact with the bodies. It takes quite a while, and we're in our astronaut gear, they can't see any compassion in our eyes, they can't see our mouth or the expression on our face—we look like robots.

When I leave, I leave the person alone with the deceased in the body bag. I know some people open the bag, the first aid and rescue teams who stay longer than us told us that. There are two kinds of firefighter trucks. Those with medical teams are only called when it's very serious.

I am assigned to a geographical area and I work in a fire station, where I answer emergency calls in 12-hour shifts. That was also very difficult, because the calls for respiratory distress never stopped.

- ## We matured with the epidemic

In the beginning, the protocol was to intubate, even if there was no respiratory distress, because blood oxygen levels were very low. Since the decision had been made by eminent doctors, we brought the patients to Intensive Care intubated. But as the epidemic progressed, we realised that those who recovered better had not necessarily been intubated. At that point, we felt we had played sorcerer's apprentice, in a way, but we didn't know it at the time. We had done what we thought best.

I remember a patient whose state I didn't find clinically alarming; he could not be moved, but he was alright with an oxygen mask. I had a long discussion with a critical care doctor on the phone, then I also talked with the SAMU (the ambulance service) which finds a place in a hospital. It was at the start of the epidemic. I didn't want to intubate. His results were not good, but I felt that his clinical state was not bad, and we were near a hospital.

My colleague who stuck to the protocol told me I had to intubate, although I thought that this patient could be helped with other techniques. We disagreed. I intubated the patient and it went well. But later, when I thought about it, I told myself that I should have stood my ground, it would have benefitted the patient. It was at the start, we were trying to find our way.

Afterwards, we intubated less and used other techniques with masks like Optiflow or Cipap that deliver a great volume of oxygen, up to 30 litres. These techniques are less invasive and allow for better recovery. When I did some work in emergency medicine at the military hospital because they needed reinforcements, we realised that these masks are very effective. In prehospital emergency care, we always deal with catastrophic situations. My colleagues and I don't dwell on them, we repress them and go on to the next case. It's one way of staying efficient; we can't become too involved in the patient's situation, or else we couldn't cope.

If I have doubts about a procedure, I ask for advice and I call back the next day. It doesn't happen often. Only in cases difficult to diagnose, or for some other reason. Of course, I get more attached to some patients, and I want to know what happened afterwards. But I see too many patients in a very bad state to ask for news each time.

• Proximity

We started out doing what we usually did, but afterwards we realised that we could not proceed as usual. As the crisis continued, we told ourselves: Be careful, bad readings don't mean you have to do invasive procedures. At first, they told us it was an organ-specific disease: respiratory, nothing but respiratory. But there was embolism and phlebitis, and neurological signs. It didn't involve the failure of just one organ, others were affected as well, like the intestine, with terrible diarrhea.

I saw a 16-year-old boy three weeks ago. I suspected Covid infection. The boy was an athlete, his father was there, and my children were about the same age. He couldn't even lift his head, his pressure was very, very low. It was just before they talked about the Kawasaki syndrome, before all the media took hold of it. I did an ultrasound, his cardiac function was severely diminished, he had had terrible diarrhea for four days. His father thought it was the Coronavirus.

He was very sick. These things make an impression on you, because you're thinking that it could be your own child. Older people don't affect you as much, it's unkind to say that. With this boy, I asked about him later, I know he is well, he came very near to needing a heart-lung machine but was able to avoid it at the last minute. He got well and will have no after-effects.

But when I arrived there was total discrepancy between the father saying: "I was told we should only call if there's respiratory distress", and a 16-year-old who can't raise his head. His room looked like my son's, who has hockey pictures on the walls; this boy was all basketball: pictures, basketball stuff everywhere. A lean young man, muscular, nice, who loved sports, and it was not normal that he couldn't raise his head, something was very wrong.

This case was also intellectually challenging because I didn't know what it was, I asked myself what was wrong with him. He also had lesions on his hands and feet, but I was unable to make the connection. I talked to the staff the next morning. My boss, who has a strong scientific bent, said it could be Kawasaki, which affects adolescents as well as children. Two days later it was all over the media. The Coronavirus can trigger this disease, but there was no Kawasaki epidemic.

I found myself in this situation because the father had had a telephone consultation where he was told that the diarrhoea was not serious. Public service announcements on television were about respiratory distress, so the father, who wanted to do the right thing, refrained from calling, since his son was breathing well. When I arrived, the situation was catastrophic.

As a parent, I would have panicked. We don't know what goes through people's minds. This father looked like a very reasonable man. When he understood that it was very serious, I saw the sudden recognition in his eyes. He said: "I didn't realise". I told him it was alright, we were there now and we would take care of his son. It was out of the question to have him sitting up in the elevator, we were risking cardiac arrest. I asked for a ladder and took him down from the second floor, it was easy and it went quickly. When he saw the ladder the father asked a lot of questions and I explained.

Of course transference takes place with my patients, but in fact I am there for a very short time. My goal is to get them to the most suitable hospital in the shortest time, with treatment initiated to avoid the worst. I am not there over the long run; the fine tuning of respiratory support is not my job.

- ## Immediacy: you do what needs to be done, and you think later

We are very tired, the shifts are very long, they last 24 hours in the truck, from 7:30 in the morning to 7:30 the next morning. At the fire station, we have to be in the truck in two or three minutes. Answering the phones is done in 12-hour shifts. We are sent off at any hour of the day or night. Sometimes at midnight, and then nothing for the rest of the night. We can sleep. Sometimes we are called out every hour or every two hours. It could be that I come back to work the following night, or I have three days off. It depends.

During the period of the Coronavirus, many of my colleagues on the medical team tested positive. It was very tiring to take their shifts if required. Although we were always in contact, there were no serious cases among us.

We have to be careful about everything we do, so we don't infect our material. In the beginning, I was rinsed down. First we had to put on the protective gear, and that took time. We're hot, we sweat, our field of vision is restricted; and we only bring the essential things into the apartment. It's a very demanding and stressful process, you must not infect other patients and you don't want to bring the virus home.

I was afraid of getting sick, since my husband was away for a year on a mission, and if I got sick, who would look after the children? I tried not to think about it. I am alone with the children and a babysitter, a young girl. Managing was already hard this year, without the Coronavirus. My work schedule is set up to allow for time with the kids. When I work nights they are sleeping. During the day, they usually go to school, except during the shutdown. But they don't see me in the evening at dinner. Now that there is no school, when I come home there is no rest. For the past six months I've had no rest. I can feel it, I'm on the brink of exhaustion. Very tired. I have to hold on until the end of June, when my husband comes back.

I also helped with the evacuation of intubated patients, by plane or by helicopters provided by the army. We were called to work on our days off. Patients were transported in Caracal helicopters and Casa planes. Doctors were needed, so there were doctors. We accompanied more than a third of the evacuations, although there are only a few of us.

The truth is, we adapted because we always do, and we always have the resources. As my husband says, when there is a need, you do it first and you think later. He is right. I did what had to be done, no problem, but we don't realise that it takes a toll on us. Like many others, we've had no rest.

•   War

I have the impression that I've lived through things more difficult than this virus. Some situations in my career were harder to take emotionally. The Coronavirus takes a toll because it goes on and on.

Once, two firemen were killed instantly in an explosion on rue de Trévise in the 9th arrondissement. I was the first doctor on the scene. It was truly a wartime scene. There was fire, stones everywhere, people screaming, human arms torn off. I don't want to lie, I found it harder than the pandemic which involves emergency medicine being delivered to sick patients.

At the front line of wars, there are screams, blood, wounds, instant death. This situation is different. We arrive, the patients are sick, we take them to Intensive Care. Of course, there is death. When cardiac arrest is due to the Coronavirus, it's impossible to resuscitate, the heart doesn't start again. But the hardest part is to see their family watch them die.

There's something I forgot to say, and talking to you reminds me. When I arrive, everyone is panicked, I am taking their loved one away and I tell them that, in any case, they can't come to the hospital. How is it possible to tell people that they won't be able to visit their loved one in the hospital, and that he may die there? Because that's the thing. And then, if he does not get out alive, you can't see the body. It's horrible.

I had suppressed all that and it comes back to me while I'm speaking with you. I found that part terrible. Now I feel better. I kept on saying: No, you can't come with us, no, you can't go to the hospital, no you won't be able to see your relative. Give me his or her cell phone and the charger. If he is not intubated, he will be able to call you; if not, you will call the ward and you will have news. It's awful, they don't know if they will ever see their loved one alive again.

• ## We are the non-existent ones

I've received no particular thanks. We are the invisible link in the system. We are not recognised, we have no caregiver bonuses, we have nothing. It's as if we don't exist in the management of Covid, when in fact we're on the front line. But as we're not part of the public hospital system (APHP) or the emergency ambulance system (SAMU), we don't count. Do you see what I mean? We are the non-existent part of the system. But in fact, we were on the front lines from the beginning.

No one talks about it. The firemen were not recognised during the crisis. At first, we were not even tested, it's the truth. And we had no bonuses, it's not a matter of money, that's not why I do my work, but for many of my colleagues it's a sign of recognition. Some of them were very frustrated; they said: "We worked many more hours than usual, we came in when it was our time off, to do the evacuations, to replace colleagues, and the shifts were particularly demanding". I myself was in a difficult situation since I had to manage everything alone at home too. The truth is that we get no recognition. It's exasperating, but that's how it is.

Of course, that's not the most important thing. I am not expecting a medal or a bonus, but for some of my colleagues it's important. They want the nation to recognise our efforts. For instance, firemen who are emergency truck drivers usually live outside the city. There was one train a day, and instead of coming in to work two days, they stayed five days without anyone acknowledging it. You see, it's rather sad. I'm talking about my ambulance driver. We are all members of the Firemen's Brigade.

In Paris, it's the army. In the region around Paris, if you call 15 or 18, depending on the area where you live, you will be sent a white truck, with a doctor, a nurse and a driver, or a red truck with a doctor, a nurse and a driver. We do exactly the same work, but those in the white truck will get the bonus, and those in the red truck won't. It's a small matter, we are used to these injustices, and because they continued over time, they became our usual lot.

- Frontline medicine

A war, yes and no. Maybe trench warfare. Now we put on protective gear less and less often. Monday, when I had to put it on again after ten days of being away, I thought: "Oh no! Here we go again". It's true, I really don't want to start this all over again. I am a bit reticent because of the psychological exhaustion.

It's war and it's not war, we surpass ourselves, we do things we wouldn't normally do, and we do them over a long period of time. In the 18th, 19th and 20th arrondissements, and in the 93 banlieue, the families come from Sub-Saharan Africa, from the Maghreb, from Asia; there are lower-middle-class families, bourgeois bohemians, working class people.

In the early days of the crisis, one of my first experiences was to be insulted by a son who was screaming at me, saying I was not doing my job for his father, who couldn't breathe. I said: "Leave the room or else I won't treat your father. Stop insulting me". He answered: "I can see your eyes, I will recognise you on the street and I'll come after you". I thought: "Does he have nothing better to do?" I also thought that he was terrified of death. His father was battered and torn, he had had a hard life, he was just about done in, not just by the Covid, if you see what I mean.

Women anaesthesiologists told you that the families were very kind. I was insulted because we did not get there fast enough, because we were not efficient enough, because we told them they couldn't go see their mother or their father. But there were also very kind families.

But you have to remember that we arrive in an emergency. They are not thinking straight. They are dumbfounded. I noticed that people rarely remember us. They remember from the point where they arrive at the hospital, but the whole period beforehand is blocked out because it was too stressful.

I know this because when I call to get news, the intern who answers says: "Oh, you are a woman!" We know that we are completely anonymous and in our overalls we are ghosts, as if were dematerialised. We arrive at a moment of crisis, they don't know who we are, and so we never have feedback. It's very rare for a patient to write us: "Thank you for saving my life".

My friends in hospital wards get little presents and letters. This never happens to me. But it's not a complaint, it has always been like that and it had to be expected even more with Covid, since they don't even see our faces. We exist without existing, but we are essential. Still, when we arrive, there is relief.

When you're too stressed, the brain stops registering things. I am aware of it when I explain what's going on. I try as much as possible to use non-medical terms with the patients. When they are conscious and I ask them to repeat what they understood, it's a disaster. You have to repeat several times. With or without a language barrier, it's the same, their stress is enormous. You don't call an ambulance to your house for nothing. When we arrive, they are panicked no matter what the problem is.

• The home front

My children ask me: "Are you tired?" They know I'll be stressed when I come home. "Did you see many Corona cases? Did you intubate?" They are 10, 11 and 13 years old and have coped well with the lockdown. They were very benevolent towards me. It was not easy, I left, I came back. I tried to be there for them as much as I could, but I can't be everywhere. They were very independent with the online learning, sometimes they had trouble, the babysitter helped them. Sometimes they would complain that I didn't take their calls when I was working. "—When I'm with a patient, I can't stop everything to solve a math problem. But there are often times when I can answer the phone". They are quite calm, and sometimes call me about an assignment. Or just to ask if they can have some screen time.

They know I am exhausted by the nightshifts. When I come home in the morning they say: "Oh, mom, you're very tired, get some sleep first". They understand now. At first, I kept doing everything like before and I did not go to sleep, but I couldn't cope without rest, so now I sleep two or three hours. They are very thoughtful: "Mommy is resting". They play, they do their school work, yoga with the babysitter, go for a walk with her; we've worked out a balance, a ritual.

I look forward to the end of June when my husband will be back. I need to slow down, to spend time with him, to have family meals, to enjoy simple pleasures. I don't need anything more.

May 28, 2020—Frontline nurses: Nanosy, Emmanuelle

• The long wait

— Emmanuelle: I am a recovery room nurse, not an Intensive Care nurse.
— Nanosy: I am a nurse anaesthetist and I usually work in the operating room.

We started out in stages. First, there was a period of preparation that lasted a week and a half to two weeks. I found that very, very long. Those two weeks were extremely stressful, since we were preparing for the unknown. I was afraid for me, for my family, I didn't know what would happen. Two whole weeks in which we prepared the ground for improvised critical care, in improvised facilities not intended for Intensive Care.

The operating room and the recovery room were transformed into primary care spaces for non-Covid patients, and the Intensive Care Unit was reserved for Covid patients. We had to get out of our comfort zone.

I worked in Intensive Care 15 years ago. Now I am coming back to it, but the procedures have changed. I had to relearn some of them. At the same time, we had to deal with a shortage of material (personal protective equipment, infusion lines, drugs).

- ## A plural body of survival

— Nanosy: After a while, everything fell into place little by little, "Little strokes fell great oaks" as the saying goes. And then the real work started. The first patients arrived. We had to go ahead, we had no choice. We stayed focused on the dressing and undressing, which are crucial before we treat patients. When we are "inside" what we are doing, we forget the "outside". And we forget to be afraid. At first, the number of basic hygiene practices kept increasing, then they became routine, they were our ritual.

This initial stage didn't last long. We got to know our colleagues from different teams. Normally, we used to see them for transfers, or during breaks, and then we went back to our respective tasks.

Since special procedures are being done in Intensive Care, we work differently with our colleagues. We're together for many hours, working hand in hand, rowing in the same boat, confronted to the same waves, a real team. We get to know each other, anaesthesiologists, nurses, caregivers, and see each other's qualities. During this difficult time, our union was our strength. We discovered wonderful people, on a personal and professional level.

Of course, we had problems involving the material. The workload, our personal and family lives were turned upside down, but these intense connections were abundant compensation.

- ## Exceptional energy

— Emmanuelle: We had 12-hour shifts several times a week, sometimes 4 or 5, alternating days, nights and week-ends, sometimes 60 hours a week.

— Nanosy: We were on the front line of this war.
— Emmanuelle: Speaking of that, we felt excited during the preparation stage when we were waiting, when everything was set up to fight the enemy, Covid. Its both physical and psychological energy. I have the impression that as long as we were emersed in it, we went on without thinking and we worked together.

Still, at some point, your body tells you that you have drained all its resources. When the first wave of the pandemic was subsiding, our energy started to drop... I personally felt intense physical exhaustion, and I slept like I never do, like when I was 20 after a birthday party, when I slept for hours on end. I have never slept so deeply for 11 or 12 hours, my body needed to recover from this trial.

— Nanosy: It was particularly hard on me because I had night shifts more often than day shifts. I was out of sync, and I still haven't recovered. But it was my decision. I had children at home and I had to make sure their schoolwork didn't suffer. But afterwards, like Emmanuelle, I felt the fatigue as the crisis was ending. I feel it now, when things are slowing down. I haven't recovered yet.

— Emmanuelle: I also feel that my sleep cycle is disturbed, I sleep very badly. It's like an emotional roller coaster, between the highs of joy produced by the teamwork, and the lows of dejection.

After the attacks in November 2015, when we treated the victims because this hospital was nearby, I felt this unity for a short time. On the ward, there was no more hierarchy, everyone was in his/her place. But this time, we had to come out of our comfort zone because some people took on jobs that were not their usual work; our confidence was altered since we are not Intensive Care nurses. Nanosy was one, but that was 15 years ago. And I never was. I think that Intensive Care is really a personal choice. You decide it's what you want to do. This type of situation is very difficult both morally and physically.

— Françoise: I know that kind of ward. My husband stayed there two months, five years before his death. The care was exceptional.

• Immediacy

— Emmanuelle: I lived through the same experience 12 years ago and 18 years ago. My father was in Intensive Care twice, for a hundred days, and it's where he died. So I was very anxious when I was transferred to work in the ICU unit, and traumatic memories came back to me. But I had no time to dwell on this, since they gave me no choice. They told me I would be an Intensive Care nurse because I had acute care skills.

And then, you don't have time to consider, you tell yourself: "Let's go!" We take care of people, we have experience. The positive side is to see how incredibly capable we are of dealing with what comes. Human beings are war machines. We tell ourselves we won't be able to do it, but in the end we can. And we worry that if there'll be a second wave we won't have the strength anymore, but I think we will. We can adapt very quickly, everyone just went ahead. It's amazing!

There's a negative side too. After my experience with the families of critical care patients, I thought a lot about those who could not visit their loved ones, and I found that very, very hard. I considered it very important to tell the patient in a coma that his family had called. I spent a lot of time transcribing these calls for them, because it was essential.

• Hope

I also heard doctors giving families very brutal news, to prevent them from hoping for what would not happen. You have probably experienced this as well, in Intensive Care doctors often tell you that "the condition is stable", they don't venture to say more as long as they're not sure of the outcome. But now, since no one knew anything about the virus, I heard more brutal words than usual, it seemed to me, to make it clear that it was serious. I was at the nurses' station when a doctor said: "There is nothing we can do to save your husband. He will probably die".

But in critical care, even when the situation is serious, you always think that a miracle can happen, something can change tomorrow, you keep going step by step; but now, this patient was pronounced terminally ill, as if nothing more could be done, when in fact he survived. There were some other reactions like that. In fact, the doctors were just as stressed as we were. I must say that they were very patient with us, when we did not know how to perform certain procedures. It's true that it was a worthwhile experience, that we hope not to see repeated too often.

• Another world

— Nanosy: A new experience, since in the recovery room and in the operating room we are rarely confronted with death. I was afraid of that and unfortunately I'm in this situation regularly since this crisis period in critical care. Intensive Care is very particular, it's really a different world.
— Emmanuelle: The instability of the patient, the risk of sudden decompensation…
— Nanosy: What's more, the disease is not well known yet, we can't predict its progression. Every day we have to adapt our procedures. We don't do things haphazardly, not at all, but sometimes we were not certain. Everyone had the same degree of knowledge at first.

— Emmanuelle: The greatest difficulty is the absence of curative care. Treating only the symptoms is frustrating for caregivers. Usually, we know that the care we provide is needed to cure the patient.
— Nanosy: All of them were admitted for the same reason: "serious Covid 19, requiring critical care"—each one with his own medical history, and pathologies other than Covid. As time went on, and this is very personal, I had the impression that I was performing the same procedures, once they were brought in: I prepared the same medications during the night, at different doses of course, I went from room to room and I did the same thing.

We tend to forget the personal stories of these patients. We stop paying attention to who they are. Especially since they've been on the ward for a long time, three of four weeks. We go into a sort of routine, we do our work, we do it well, but I had the impression that I was repeating the same gestures over and over, always the same tasks. I realised this near the end.

• Laughter

— Emmanuelle: And we speak to them, since patients hear us even in a coma. I noticed I was speaking all the time, a little like you. I talk to them a lot. I'll never forget what I said to one patient. The ventilator was ringing loudly and I didn't know why. I tried to fix the machine, I thought the breathing tube was clogged, I tried to clear it, but it kept on ringing. It lasted at least five minutes and five minutes is a long time when a machine is ringing next to your ears.

Finally, I said to the patient: "Look here, Mister So-and-so"—I remember his name very well, he was in a coma—"that will do! we have to end this craziness! And I promise I will buy you a drink when you leave the hospital". And the ventilator stopped ringing. Of course, I must have done something that worked, but still, the whole thing made us laugh, we laughed so much, it was very funny.
— Françoise: Like in Charlie Chaplin's slapsticks movies and other films made after the First World War, where everything collapses all the time and everyone laughs.
— Emmanuelle: We had joyful moments like that, situations that are not normally funny, but became hilarious in that context.

• Difficult awakening

— Nanosy: Despite everything, we were able to awaken patients, to take them off the machine, and have the satisfaction of accomplishing our task. We forget the routine; once they are no longer in a coma, it's different.

— Françoise: Franck was saying that they are transferred to another ward then.

— Nanosy: In Intensive Care, when the patient's state allows it, we stop the sedation and we wean them off the ventilator. We assess his or her neurological status (consciousness, agitation, orientation, verbal responses, motor responses). Sometimes the patient does very well at first but becomes exhausted after several hours; in that case, we go back to the previous procedures (sedation and artificial respiration). This stage can last a few hours or a few days.

Once the patient is stable and sufficiently awake, breathing on his own (spontaneous ventilation) while still hooked up to the ventilator, we go ahead with the extubation (taking out the breathing tube and removing the ventilator), so that he can breathe on his own. Once patients are off the machine, and their condition is satisfactory, they are transferred to other wards for follow-up care and rehabilitation.

When they wake up, they are often confused at first, lost. Sometimes they go through a delusional period, they have hallucinations. The awakening can be peaceful, but it can also be agitated.

We talk to them normally, and we bring them back to the present context: "You're in the hospital, today is such-and-such a day, it's noon, I am the nurse looking after you today..." The time it takes them to find their bearings varies. For some, it's a few days, for others a few weeks.

— Emmanuelle: We speak to them a lot, but sometimes we forget while we have to concentrate on dangerous medications, on catheters. The syringe relay procedure has to be done very carefully. After that, the relation with the patient takes precedence again, and we talk. Each of us says whatever he wants. There were times when the patient was probably not listening to me, because they also need to rest, but you have to remember that when they sleep they still hear us.

•   Writing

— Nanosy: We kept a log, a little diary for each patient. The caregivers fill them although it is not mandatory, so that patients will know what happened during their stay in Intensive Care. We don't record medical data, but write things like: "I looked after you today, Sir. You are doing a little better and we were able to stop the sedation. You're making progress! The doctor called your wife to give her news".

— Emmanuelle: The diaries were created in Intensive Care Units because post-Intensive Care patients went through a phase of depression related to the black hole left by the coma. The logs are written for the patients by caregivers who describe everyday life in the Unit, explaining what happened to them over several weeks or months, in an effort to prevent post-traumatic symptoms.

— Françoise: My husband had delusions. I was surprised to see how appropriately the nurses reacted. Psychoanalysts should train here, where one is close to what matters most, life itself. In addition to dispensing routine care, you are witnesses to moments without a witness.

— Nanosy: It's true, in that sense, yes. Moreover, the diary is also meant for the patient's family. In case of death, it will be a memory of what their loved ones went through while the family could not visit them. Perhaps it will help them to go on from there.

— Emmanuelle: It's especially important for patients who were transferred. You get Covid in Paris and you wake up somewhere in Brittany, far from everyone, and you're even most lost.

• Simplicity and return to life

— Emmanuelle: Personally, I didn't take the time to write these logs. My father, who later died in Intensive Care, had been traumatised and went through a post-hospitalisation depression after he was in Intensive Care the first time, due to this experience. We told him what state he had been in only afterwards, since he had almost no memory of it at all. This left me with a fear of saying the wrong things, and I thought that you could use an inappropriate word, a word which might harm the patient... and I didn't want to risk it.

— Nanosy: We used a lot of restraint in what we wrote, we were careful, we didn't write everything. We kept in mind that the log would be read later.

— Emmanuelle: Some things are important to know, others are not worth bothering with. And we have to use terms everyone can understand, as our jargon can be anxiety provoking for the patient and his family.

— Françoise: Who had the idea of keeping a log?

— Emmanuelle: It's a tool they use here at the hospital, in Intensive Care.

— Nanosy: Initially it came from the Pitié-Salpêtrière Hospital. It's an important tool. By writing, you project yourself into the future: one day he will read it, one day his wife or his children will want to know about what he went through. And that gives us hope that maybe he'll get well.

— Emmanuelle: As far as I'm concerned, I didn't have time. I was not familiar with Intensive Care procedures, and there was so much to learn and to do. Writing in the diary was not a priority, when you had to provide vital care.

— Nanosy: What I remembered best was the patients' first names, not out of lack of respect but because they were like my family. I still remember the 7 names. There were 7 beds, not many new arrivals as the Unit was full and patients stayed several weeks. In the operating room we sometimes call them by their first names to wake them up, because they respond better and seem to be less lost when they regain consciousness. I kept this habit with Covid patients.

— Emmanuelle: I was struck by the fact that we adopted "our" patients. Often, when I was home at night I thought of them and I told myself: "People thank us with their applause, what we're doing is not easy physically or emotionally, there are ups and downs". But I couldn't imagine myself anywhere else. We were in the right place. Nothing would have made me want to get away, to be somewhere where I couldn't look after them.

No particular patient evoked my sympathy more than another, because we made the same effort for all of them, regardless of their age. We gave the best of ourselves.

— Françoise: Did they suffer a great deal? Usually they tell that to the nurse. What was difficult for you? We're going to talk about the difficult things.

• Sensory impressions

— Emmanuelle: For me, the hardest thing was to aspirate them all the time.

— Nanosy: There was something specific, I don't know if you noticed it, Emmanuelle, there was a smell—Emmanuelle nods—a Covid smell. I'm sorry, if you had smelled it you'd know, it's indescribable. It was not the smell of feces or of vomit, but a very particular odour you could call nauseating. They had the same smell. It came mostly from their mouth or from the breathing tube—the tube inserted through the mouth into the trachea to allow artificial respiration. We do a lot of ENT procedures, especially involving the mouth. I have the impression that that smell is still sticking to me.

— Emmanuelle: At night I would wash, but the smell stayed.

— Nanosy: I don't know what it is. I was also looking after patients who didn't have Covid, and they didn't have the same smell. It was pervasive, it stuck to you. Not when they arrived, but when the disease had taken hold, in the unstable phase, when they were on a respirator with internal feeding by gastric tube, and they had different kinds of catheters.

— Emmanuelle: we never talked about it. Just mentioning it now makes me smell it.

• Suffocating with them

— Nanosy: Even on the respirator, they have a lot of trouble breathing, adjusting to the machine. As soon as there is the smallest movement or change of position during the daily care, they suffer, they can't breathe. I had the impression that I was suffocating with them.

— Emmanuelle: They drown, they secrete so much mucus, they're so full of it, like in acute pulmonary oedema, they froth at the mouth, despite the breathing tube, it's like snail slime.

There were times when I broke down outside the room. You spend an hour with the patient to do all the procedures, you aspirate him and relieve him of all his respiratory difficulties, once, twice, three times, and you're ready to leave. You're wearing protective gear and you follow the procedure to get it off. Then you see your patient through the glass in the door exactly as he was before. And I have flung my protective clothing away thinking: "I'm sick of this Covid!" You take one step forward and two steps back. Usually, when you leave the room, your patient is perfectly clean. But with these patients, you look through the glass and you think: "I haven't done anything".

— Nanosy: Another hard thing is the dressing and undressing, as required by the protocol: hand washing, hair cap, goggles, FFP2 mask, lab coat, apron, gloves. This suiting up becomes a ritual, but it takes time. Once you're dressed, you mustn't forget anything—material, medications, procedures—because if you do, you'll have to repeat the dressing from the beginning. Like Emmanuelle said, we spend time providing the care, and we realise we have to start over as if we hadn't done anything, and sometimes we get discouraged.

— Emmanuelle: It is a period of stagnation. We had to turn the patient over onto his belly for 16 hours a day, and then turn him back on his back for 8 hours.

— Nanosy: It takes 7 people to turn a patient over: one to hold his head, 3 on one side and 3 on the other. We count: 1, 2, 3 and we turn him, just like soldiers, paying attention to the different devices to which he is attached: respirator, dialysis machine, catheters, feeding tube…, and checking his tolerance for the new position. This procedure relies on a well-established technique, carried out by qualified and experienced medical staff.

All the Covid patients in Intensive Care had severe respiratory distress syndrome. Turning them over, when not contraindicated, increases the chance of survival, improves gas exchange and redistributes perfusion towards better ventilated pulmonary areas.

— Emmanuelle: When we turn them over, we change the sheets at the same time.

— Nanosy: The physical care includes many tasks: preventing scarring, changing dressings if needed, basic care, oral hygiene twice as often as usual, eye care. Nutritional and hydration needs are provided for by infusions and the gastric tube. Hydration is kept a little low.

— Françoise: My husband was scribbling "o"s on a pad. I thought he had forgotten how to write. When he was able to speak, he told me he was asking for water ("*eau*" in French).

• Your presence when they die alone

— Nanosy: We don't see them completely recovered when they leave this ward. We don't know what happens afterwards, if they regain complete respiratory and cognitive functions. They don't go straight home, but spend time in another ward. The doctors know the follow-up story but we don't have time to discuss their recovery. We just carry on.

— Françoise: The emergency doctor of the fire brigade didn't have any news either.

— Emmanuelle: This is how things are set up. We look after them for a while, and after that I imagine what I wish about them, about their life, not their death.

— Françoise: Since you brought it up, you were saying that the hardest thing is their death.

— Emmanuelle: The number of patients who died in such a short time.

— Nanosy: There is a very specific protocol. We place them in a double body bag for fear of contagion. Care of the body after unplugging everything is not a pleasant task, but we have no choice.

— Emmanuelle: Our patients were all very sick, we were more or less expecting it, we saw some of them get worse little by little. We sense it when the body collapses, their complexion takes on a purple tone.

— Nanosy: We know this, and it's my greatest worry. I tell myself: "I hope it doesn't happen during my shift, I'm not ready for it." A death is always difficult to accept.

— Emmanuelle: An additional difficulty is seeing them die alone. We're there, of course, but we don't consider ourselves their family, and it's extremely distressing. So many people died alone...

— Nanosy: And, on the other hand, there are the families that can't see them.

— Emmanuelle: It was unprecedented, since in Intensive Care families are always able to come. But not now.

— Nanosy: When it happens, it's hard to take, yet we go on, we take care of the other patients. But I still remember their faces, it's not so much their death that stays with me. It's special, I Don't know how else to say it.

— Emmanuelle: It's part of our work. We're lucky to have a certain distance, since we don't know them.

— Françoise: I will tell you a story. Laurence Sterne, an 18th-century author, who was also a pastor called to the bedside of the dying, wrote in his novel *Tristram Shandy* that he wished his last moments to be spent not at home, where "the concern of my friends [...] will crucify my soul", but in the presence of a professional person, reassuring and attentive. He died in 1768, according to his wish. I am telling you this because you were there.

• Absence of ritual

— Emmanuelle: I was not confronted with the death of Covid patients, but there were also many deaths among other patients during the same period. Two sections were created: Covid and non-Covid, and I went from one to the other.

Critical care patients came from everywhere, because Intensive Care Units were overburdened. Most deaths among these patients occurred in our hospital. One family member was allowed to come to the hospital with them. It was terrible. Usually, people don't die in an operating room, now reserved for non-Covid patients. I saw a child who stayed with his mother until her last breath. He spent the night waiting for his mother in a large, cold room not intended for this. He screamed out of pain and fear when she died. Everyone heard his scream.

It's true that we were there for those who were alone. I see the care of the body after death differently. It's not a pleasant task, it's not the care I prefer to provide, but I consider it—perhaps I'm lying to myself—a moment when the stress of acute care is replaced with peacefulness and respect of the body. I make them beautiful for the family, I talk to them, I try to turn this passage into something less negative.

— Nanosy: There is care after death for Covid patients. Then we place them in a double body bag. The family doesn't come to see the body, which is taken to the morgue after the administrative process is completed: attestation of death, death certificates, issuing a registration number.

— Françoise: There is no ritual, as there is in all human societies around the world. Where are you from, Nanosy?

• **Body-turning ceremony in Madagascar**

— Nanosy: I'm from Madagascar, where there are burials like in Western countries, and also special funeral rites: *Famadihana*, or ancestral custom practiced especially in the Central Highlands. The family asks for the benediction and protection of the ancestors, then the bodies are exhumed and wrapped in new shrouds before being placed back in the family tomb.

— Françoise: How often?

— Nanosy: This rite is becoming rarer these days, because it has become too expensive; it takes place once or twice in a generation. I participated in it for the first time last year. After speaking and asking the ancestors for their benediction, the bodies are identified by a photograph or some other object which have been put next to them. Then they are wrapped in their beautiful new shroud made of raw silk, exactly as our elders described it. Up to a hundred bodies can be placed in the family tomb. They are placed in a specific order.

— Françoise: William Rivers, a British neurologist and anthropologist turned psychoanalyst when he was drafted during the First World War to treat traumatised officers. He had previously lived among the head hunters of the Solomon Islands, to study their funeral rites, as foreign to us as those you mentioned, Nanosy. To help his patients, he remembered the words of his informer Nijiru, whom he considered a formidable therapist. And he wondered about the gradual disappearance of these practices under the pressure of civilisation, and how it compared with the absence of funeral rites for the young men massively killed by the war.

You started our discussion with a proverb: "Little strokes fell great oaks". I read a little book by Jean Paulhan, *L'expérience du proverbe*[2] (The Experience of the Proverb), which describes how proverbs are used in Madagascar.

Emmanuelle concluded our discussion with another saying: "There is no such thing as chance".

These testimonies go beyond the contradiction they bring to light: "It's war and it's not war"; they resonate with a frontline psychotherapy characteristic of wartime. The subtitles I used are partly based on Thomas Salmon's principles for what was called during the First World War "forward psychiatry": proximity, immediacy, hope and simplicity.

Notes

1 During the two hours when I was looking after her, her heart stopped, and they were praying for their mother.
2 Paulhan, J., *L'expérience du proverbe*, Bordeaux: L'échoppe, 1993.

Part 2

Frontline Psychotherapy

Aside from the four principles referred to in the testimonies in Part 1, three recurring themes remain present as we continue from the first to the second part of this book.

DOI: 10.4324/9781003257592-2

Chapter 1

Witnessing Events without a Witness

Whether we are talking about caregivers on the front lines, be it in emergency medicine and Critical Care or in crowded military hospitals, we must simply acknowledge the intelligence that makes survival possible in this "unimaginable time of war", without further comment. British psychoanalyst Wilfred Bion formulates the knowledge at stake in such circumstances when, based on his experience as a veteran of the First World War, he speaks of "thoughts without a thinker", in search of a thinker to think them. Provided that this other—for instance, an analyst—expresses his impressions in the interaction, instead of hiding behind a wall of silence and diagnoses.

Among those who have faced death, this intelligence records, in a sensory memory, silenced traces of catastrophes that may have happened over generations. Analysts working with abandoned babies or immigrant children told me that when they tell them what little they know of their histories and the countries where their parents come from,[1] they progressively come out of withdrawal. Otherwise, this type of memory persists, to show what cannot be said, until it eventually encounters an other who "testifies to events without a witness". This expression was first used by Dori Laub,[2] analyst at Yale and co-founder of the Fortunoff Video Archives for Holocaust Testimonies.

For him, the emergence of an alterity in the place where all otherness had been destroyed took place in a session with his analyst, which brought back the 6-year-old boy deported in 1942 to a camp in Romania. Laub's analysis took place while he was in training at Austen Riggs, a clinic dedicated to the analysis of psychoses, in Stockbridge, Massachusetts.

While he was recounting to his Swedish analyst how "on a beautiful summer day he sat with a little girl on the banks of the Burg River which ran along the camp", the analyst quoted the remark of a Theresienstadt inmate when the Swedish liberated the camp: "The Soviets brought us breakfast in bed". The phrase was a reference to the 1944 Nazi propaganda film *Theresienstadt: A Documentary Film*, produced for the visit of a Red Cross delegation. "At that moment", Laub says, "a door opened onto the horror of my own history, and I saw the tortures of the camp". The analyst, acting as

DOI: 10.4324/9781003257592-3

a witness, "resuscitated" the breath that liberates speech, which had been muffled where no other was present.

One of the rare survivors of that camp, in 1950 Dori Laub immigrated with his mother to Israel, where "we had to move forward and forget the past". He studied psychology, and then medicine at Yale, and was drafted to serve in the Yom Kippur War. Working as a psychiatrist, he discovered in traumatised soldiers the same cut-out unconscious. "In these children of concentration camp survivors, unspoken memories were revived by the violence on the battlefield". This is what made Laub decide "to become the one who can tell another person: 'I am with you in the very process in which you think the other has been lost. I am your witness'". This phrase defines the scope of the testimonies I recorded.

The psychotherapy of trauma is as old as wars and tends to disappear during the "long week-end" between catastrophes, to use Bion's expression. In that context, the injunction that prevails is: "Forget all that, it's in the past". But what are we to do with a memory that doesn't forget, manifested through symptoms, Laub says, "that show into advanced age an intelligence whose cognitive and emotional maturity is not at all that of the child who underwent such trials"? Nor, we might add, is it that of the adult whose life it disturbs. In this context, Wilfred Bion speaks of "premature knowledge", whose untimely emergence is labelled mental illness by narrow minds.

Notes

1 I learned this from Monique Braoude, child analyst, and Maylis de la Saussay, analyst of babies abandoned at birth.
2 Laub, D. (1937–2018). Une clinique de l'extrême, Le Coq-Héron, 2015, No. 220–221, Erès; Entretien avec Françoise Davoine (interview), Le Coq-Héron, 2013, No. 214, p. 145. In the interview, Dori Laub describes the start of his project in 1979, and its subsequent development.

Chapter 2

The Role of Coincidences

"Suddenly, with some patients, something changes and they are better", when nothing predicted it, Lucie said. In the same way, the psychotherapy of madness and trauma can suddenly be marked by a decisive session—this is what happened to Dory Laub—breaking through the routine that Emmanuelle called "stagnation".

The sudden emergence of scenes or events through uncanny repetition is characteristic of wartime, when time stops owing to the destruction of symbolic bearings. Causality—which relies on the past for the cause and on the future for the effect—being rendered ineffectual, chance acquires a considerable role. "I am only alive owing to chance", we often hear people say. In that context one has to "hold on", because "a miracle can always happen", Emmanuelle said, shocked by the fatal prognosis given by the doctor to a patient's family, "when in fact the patient survived".

The testimonies underscore the temporal "apartness" in which therapy takes place, and express apprehension about the closing of that parentheses. Franck fears that: "Now we will go back to normal life". "–I hope we will not lose this new team spirit" says Lucie, and Jessica confirms: "We built closer relations by caring for Covid patients together. I want them to last". Anne Lise also comments: "We did things we were not used to doing". Emmanuelle looks ahead: "We worry that if there'll be a second wave we won't have the strength…, but I think we will". And Nanosy adds: "When we're working, we forget everything else".

La Fontaine depicted the specific time of a pandemic in *The Animals Ill with the Plague*[1]:

> The sorest ill that Heaven hath […] —
> The plague (to call it by its name,)
> Waged war on beasts, both wild and tame

But instead of raising a hue and cry against a scapegoat—the donkey, in the fable—and despite their fear, which all those I interviewed acknowledged as well, they discovered unsuspected resources in themselves, both physical

DOI: 10.4324/9781003257592-4

and psychological. Claude Barrois,[2] psychoanalyst and former medical director of the psychiatric at the Val de Grâce military hospital in Paris, defines courage as "the margin for action left by fear".

In this regard, I can't resist referring to an interview with Edmund Hillary, who succeeded in climbing to the top of Mount Everest in 1953. When he was asked, at the end of his life, what he felt as he approached the summit, he answered simply: "Fear", adding: "I could only continue climbing". As they carry out their work, those whom we applauded at 8 o'clock every evening don't see themselves as heroes either. Rather, their question is, how to tell the outside world, which is so saturated with frightful news, that in their work there is not only fear, but also joy, when, suddenly, the patient is better and he can be weaned from the machine?

Faced with the injunction quoted by Dori Laub: "It's all in the past, don't think about it anymore", the memory that recorded the intensity of wartime disagrees. Unbeknownst to us, it asks, during peace time, that the intelligence it deployed to survive catastrophes be acknowledged.

Notes

1 La Fontaine, J. (1678). The Animals Ill with the Plague, in *The Complete Fables of Jean de La Fontaine*, N. R. Shapiro (trans.), Chicago: University of Illinois Press, 2007, p. 156.
2 Barrois, C., *Psychanalyse du guerrier*, New York: Hachette, 1993.

Chapter 3

The Limits of Mainstream Psychoanalysis

I will now follow the path taken by this memory in my own case, until it crossed that of the anaesthesiologists, nurses and emergency doctors I interviewed on the front lines, reviving a feminine agency which drove me to become a psychoanalyst in the psychiatric hospital, although my studies had been in neither psychology nor psychiatry, but in classical literature and sociology. What's more, I only became acquainted with Freud in the summer of 1968 when I read *Introduction to Psychoanalysis*,[1] and immediately started psychoanalysis. That's when I got the idea of becoming an analyst in a public psychiatric hospital.

In the meantime, I had fallen on my head while climbing the Dame Jeanne rock in the forest of Fontainebleau. When I came out of the coma, I realised that Jeanne was the name of my paternal grandmother, native of the Bauges, whom I had been forbidden to meet. The Dame of the rock had revived the fossilised memory of this craziness, which the child I had been could not understand. After that fall, I started to wonder about the psychoanalysis of madness, that Freud, at the end of the *Introduction*, dismisses in two perfunctory sentences:

> Observation shows that persons suffering from narcissistic neuroses have no capacity for transference, or only insufficient remains of it. They reject the physician not with hostility, but with indifference.
>
> I was no further ahead when I read Lacan, whose seminars I was attending. Indeed, at the end of his *On a Question Preliminary to Any Possible Treatment of Psychosis*,[2] he foregoes dealing with the question of transference in this context, "because there can be no question of [going] 'beyond Freud' when post-Freud psychoanalysis has gone back to an earlier stage."

Little by little, I met other analysts and authors who did not comply with this limitation. Most had worked in wartime and had described this transference in clinical texts or works of fiction. I shall introduce them in turn, asking the reader to forgive me if their quick overview under my pen will

DOI: 10.4324/9781003257592-5

make this book resemble the movie *Hellzapoppin*,[3] filmed during the Second World War, where a group of Native Americans on horseback bursts in on the scene several times, in a manner totally unconnected to the plot.

In fact, in the middle of this hubbub, you hear the songs and the dances of Sioux Indians, whom we had a chance to meet on the Rosebud reservation in South Dakota. At their request, we invited them to France in 1985—medicine man Joe Eagle Elk, his assistant Stanley Red Bird and a few others—, to speak about their ceremonial medicine, at the École des Hautes Études in Paris and at the Maison de la Culture in Reims.

But let us go back to the starting point of the research that led to all these encounters.

Notes

1 Freud, S. (1916–1917). *Introduction to Psychoanalysis*, Chicago, IL: Independent Publishing, 2020.
2 Lacan, J., On a Question Preliminary to Any Possible Treatment of Psychosis, in *Écrits: A Selection*, A. Sheridan (Trans.), London: Tavistock/Routledge, 1977.
3 *Hellzapoppin*, film, Potter, H. C. (dir), 1941.

Chapter 4

Starting Point

From the Personal to the Social

On the traces of war

At the end of 1968 I joined Alain Touraine's sociology laboratory, later re-named the Centre for the Study of Social Movements. At the start of the 1970s, Jean-Max Gaudillière and I undertook a research project called "Madness and the Social Link", which was the topic of the weekly seminars I mentioned earlier. Our field of research was the psychiatric hospital where we eventually became psychoanalysts. Thus, our seminars took place at the crossroads of these two disciplines. But why had we embarked on this particular path? We could not have said.

The occasion arose in 1973 at a meeting of the *École freudienne* founded by Jacques Lacan, where we met Edmond Sanquer, head of a psychiatric department. At our request, he consented to have us join his staff, and he asked us to meet him in front of his building in Paris at 5 o'clock the next morning. This was the start of our trips—at first daily and then weekly, to the Prémontré psychiatric hospital in the North East of France.[1]

The road to Prémontré cut through cemeteries filled with white crosses as far as the eye could see. We saw them every day without paying attention. The "residents", who had been in the hospital for years, spoke of war all the time. Not surprising, in that region called "département de l'Aisne", which had been regularly devastated by conflicts since the Franco-Prussian war of 1870. And then the war came to life for me. One day, I was sitting in the common room of the ward with mister H, who had been admitted in the aftermath of the Second World War. Pipe in hand, holding his pipe, he was telling me about the circumstances of his hospitalisation.

The following night I saw my maternal grandfather in a dream, with his pipe—resembling Mister H's. He had been a stretcher-bearer in the Great War. I knew that. But it took me a long time to open a book about his division,[2] published in 1919 and dedicated by name to the survivors. Long after this dream, I discovered that he had served on several front lines including, no doubt, those along the route to Prémontré. He never spoke about it, but he whistled military airs and other tunes to me, saying only: "I was a

DOI: 10.4324/9781003257592-6

stretcher-bearer because I was in the band". He belonged to the band of his small town, Champlitte, in the eastern province of Franche Comté.

Another memory of this grandfather hospitalised in his later years came back to me. After he went away, diagnosed with something incomprehensible called atherosclerosis, I always imagined him with his hands gripping bars. While he was gone, my grandmother spoke to herself and I used to tell my playmates: "No, no, there is someone with her".

When he came home to die, I was ten. Happy to see me again, he asked for his trumpet to play something for me. But the grown-ups refused, exchanging looks that implied he had lost his head. Never mind! He went ahead and whistled his tune to me with the skill men used to have before recordings. After that, he was taken to his room and died a short time later. Long afterwards, I inherited the trumpet and the bugle he had brought back from the front, badly dented.

This suppressed story probably prompted me to travel the road leading to Mister H, who on that day acted as a therapist, reversing our roles momentarily, as described by analysts of madness and trauma. On that occasion, a "surviving image"—that Aby Warburg calls *"nachleben"*, or after-life—allowed the emergence of a narrative, in a specific type of transference.

"Transference" is a word used in the testimonies of those I interviewed, although they do not mention psychoanalysis. Jessica sees herself intubated in a nightmare; she connects this with her transference to a dying patient of her age and of similar origins. Anne Lise experiences transference with a young boy the age of her son, and Lucie feels afraid until she actually connects with her patients.

In this context, I use the term "plural body", created in situations of extreme danger, whose capacities surpass those of the individual. Franck stressed the unexpected link created by a "positive dynamic" around the patients, regardless of each professional's status.

Plural body of survival

The term "plural body" came to my mind when I read psychoanalyst Maria Landau's article "Les enfants de Terezin"[3] (The Children of Terezin). She wrote it after reading about Anna Freud's experience[4] when, in October 1945, she took in 6 three-year-old Jewish orphans rescued from the camp of Teresienstadt, in a country house located in Sussex.

At first, the child analyst was disheartened to see that her project was failing, since these children kept destroying the pretty interior of the house, breaking the toys and insulting the nursemaids rudely in German.

Still, she observed that it was impossible to separate them from each other, and she noted an unusual detail. At the age when "me first" behaviour is to be expected, a child who had a cake to share kept the smallest part for himself, in order to nourish their leaderless plural body and ensure their collective survival.

A second setback occurred when they gradually established a bond with a particular person, learned to speak English and fell seriously ill. But little by little, through contact with adults ready to confront deathly violence and to remain present when the children were on the brink of death, they entered the sphere of social relations. In Antiquity, a name was given to this special transference, which at first tied them to each other and later to an adult.

Therapon, the second in combat, in charge of funeral rites

By calling our seminar "Madness and the Social Link", we avoided using the word "psychosis", which is associated with an irreversible psychic structure. Since the word "trauma" was not yet in fashion, we spoke of catastrophes explored by madness "at the intersection of world history with personal history", as a patient said about his delusions. This was also the teaching of the authors we read each year in the seminar.

For instance, Japanese writer Kenzaburo Oe answers the plea: *Teach Us to Outgrow Our Madness* in his book *The Silent Cry*, where the transference between two brothers makes it possible to reveal incest long kept silent, as well as disastrous political events, cut out of the family history for a century, and dating back to the Meiji Restoration.

Another winner of the Nobel Prize for literature, like Oe, Afro-American writer Toni Morrison, in her novel *Beloved*,[5] portrays the madness of a runaway slave haunted by the ghost of the little daughter she killed to save her from slavery. The novel ends to the rhythm of a chorus of former slaves, as they are taking her back into the community.

Don Quixote,[6] regularly defeated after fighting surviving images of "his father" Cervantes's war and enslavement, recovers each time thanks to his talking cure with Sancho Panza. Contradicting the tenet: "no transference in psychosis", these literary works bring what is impossible to say into language play, provided an other is involved in recovering lost breath and speech.

The name of this other—*therapôn*—is given in the *Iliad*,[7] which passed down the Trojan war orally for two centuries, to the rhythm of dactylic hexameters, before it was put in writing in the 6th-century BC. The *therapon*—Patroclus for Achilles—is the second in combat, and the "ritual double" in charge of funeral duties. This is the nature of the bond between Roland and Oliver in *The Song of Roland*,[8] between Sancho Panza and Don Quixote, and between Corporal Trim and Captain Toby in Laurence Sterne's *Tristram Shandy*,[9] the 18th-century novel inspired by Cervantes's masterpiece.

The therapeutic power of this agency in literature is illustrated by a story told by Sterne's biographer.[10] A partisan of the abolition of slavery, Sterne was writing a passage on that issue in the last volume of his novel—after the others had been published—when he received a letter from a former slave named Ignatius Sancho, who wrote:

> I am one of those people whom the vulgar [...] call "Negurs". [...] I am [...] indebted to you for the character of your amiable uncle Toby. I declare, I would walk ten miles in the dog-days, to shake hands with the honest corporal.

I immediately recognised the function of *therapon* in the six-voice testimonies I will now follow up by recounting my adventures in search of a psychotherapy of madness and trauma. As I was wondering how to go about this, Boccaccio came to my rescue. I had been reading his *Decameron*[11] during the confinement, a book addressed to "most gracious ladies".

Psychotherapy during the plague in Florence

Boccacio was 35 when the Black Plague devastated Europe and broke out in Florence, where he lived, in 1348. He spent the next three years writing the *Decameron*, whose Introduction speaks to us today:

> Between March and July of that year, because of the ferocity of the pestilence [...] one hundred thousand human creatures [were] killed off within the walls of the city of Florence. [...] If I were not one of many people who saw it with their own eyes, I would scarcely have dared to believe it [...], even if I had heard it from a completely trustworthy person.

Physicians understood nothing. The stench of bodies was everywhere. The "reverend authority of the laws" collapsed. Some people went into confinement: "Having withdrawn, living separate from everybody else, they settled down and locked themselves in [...], refusing news of the dead or the sick..." Others gave themselves over to unbridled debauchery. "The ordeal had so withered the hearts of men that families broke apart", and "what is even more incredible and cruel, mothers and fathers abandoned their children". Many people left the city to take refuge in the country. "As for the lesser people [...], they presented the most miserable spectacle". Funeral rites disappeared. "Many people [...] passed away from this life without anyone there to witness it at all".

In this setting, seven young women between 18 and 28, dressed in the sombre garb of mourning, are gathered by chance one Tuesday evening in the Church of Santa Maria Novella. They know each other and seat themselves in a circle. The most resolute, Pampinea, decides to shake off their lethargy and defend their right to live by getting away from the sight of the sick and the dead, from the criminals who roam the city in packs, "scoffing at the laws", and from constant news that "'Such an one is dead' or 'Such an one is at the point of death'". They are left alone in their homes, terrified by "the ghosts of the departed". Pampinea admonishes them, asking: "What look we for? What dream we? Why are we [...] sluggish [...] to provide for our safety?" She tells them that they can escape to the countryside: "It's a matter of will".

She urges them to think of their "joie de vivre" among the natural delight of a country estate, "if death should not first overtake us". The others are ready to leave at once, except Filomena who is more realistic about the risk to their safety. Just then, "Fortune" brings three young men into the church; these gallant gentlemen are their friends and agree to accompany them.

Once they arrive at their refuge, far from the general chaos, a form of governance is established, to be scrupulously respected for two weeks. Each day, a queen or a king will be designated, who will take responsibility for the material and psychological welfare of the company.

A veritable psychotherapy is put in place, perhaps the oldest in the world, consisting of telling stories and regaining breath in conditions of suffocating fear. The stories were told in the afternoon; a song followed, and then dancing and singing accompanied on a lute, a viola, and even a bagpipe. There were strolls in the enchanting countryside before meals, discussions and more songs, punctuating each day which "passed like its predecessor".

Every day, except Saturday and Sunday, the ten young people take turns telling a story on a subject chosen in advance the previous evening by the queen or the king. In the space of two weeks, these stories constitute the hundred "novellas" of the *Decameron*, a term signifying ten days in Greek.

The book starts and ends with two stories that present the political context in which the young people are carrying out their project: the breakdown of law and order. The first story portrays a notary who takes pride in circumventing the law and getting away with crimes. At the end of his life, he must confess in order to obtain a decent burial. True to his character, he tricks the old friar who comes to confess him, although the holy man's wisdom is held in great esteem. And so, the crooked notary dies with the reputation of having been a saintly man.

The same perversion is found in the last story, but this time the heroine nullifies its effect. Her name is Griselda and she will become, in subsequent centuries, the heroine of several operas.[12] Boccaccio's Griselda, a girl of humble origins, becomes the wife of a marquis. She is obedient and devoted to her husband, until he decides to put her to a sadistic test. He takes her two small children away from her and makes her believe that they are dead. He treats her like a slave and finally sends her back to her father, so that he can marry a woman of his rank.

Griselda says nothing, asks no questions and does not try to understand. She keeps her dignity. By refusing to enter the zone of death into which her husband is luring her, she subverts his scheme, is reunited with her adolescent children and regains her position in the household. This silent resistance is like that shown by the young people in *The Decameron*, who return to Florence fortified by having constituted a plural body of survival. According to Hannah Arendt,[13] all debate with a murderous agency is absurd. "The only valid argument [...] is promptly to rescue the person whose death is predicted".

Like Boccaccio, I will spell out the theme of my stories, in capital letters: STORIES TOLD ON THE PATH TO THE WAR WAGED BY FRONT-LINE PSYCHOTHERAPY. And I will start with a song.

Ring around the rosie

I came to know this nursery rhyme as I watched my American grandchildren dance in a circle with their friends:

> Ring around the rosie,
> A pocket full of posies,
> Ashes, ashes, ashes,
> We all fall down.

While the children dropped to the ground bursting with laughter, Dyani, their mother, explained that this ditty referred to plague epidemics in London, going at least as far back as the 14th century. A rosy rash around the mouth was the first sign of the disease, people carried herbs to ward off the stench of pestilence, corpses were burned on funeral pyres, and people were falling dead all around.

Although learned minds might contest the origin of the nursery rhyme, I thought of it when Nanosy and Emmanuelle dared to speak of the persistent odour which they could still smell by simply talking about it. The spots on the skin, flowers in a pocket to smell under the mask, the ashes of corpses given no funeral rites, and people dropping to the ground dead are familiar images now. The rhymes sung by dancing children are a memory whose metaphors have to be taken literally again. In wartime, words regain the physical consistency of things.

This process at work in delusions, where, according to British psychoanalyst Wilfred Bion, "thoughts are things and things are thoughts", calls for a co-researcher with whom to think them. When Freud was elaborating the psychoanalysis of trauma with Joseph Breuer, he made the same observation in his *Project for a Scientific Psychology*, written in pencil on a train in 1895,[14] on his way back from a visit to Berlin, to his friend, otorhinolaryngologist Wilfred Fliess: namely that the "primary process" where words are taken for things is distinct from the "secondary process" where words can flow freely.

Then, suddenly, in 1898, he put an end to his collaboration with Breuer. What happened?

Notes

1 Davoine, F., *Mother Folly: A Tale*, Stanford, CA: Stanford University Press, 2014.
2 Humbert, Capitaine, *La Division Barbot*, New York: Hachette, 1919.
3 Landau, M. (1990). Les enfants de Terezin, in *Le temps du non: Psychanalyse et Idéologie* 5: 45–51.
4 Freud, A. and Dann, S. (1951). An Experiment in Group Upbringing, in *Psychoanalytic Study of the Child* 6: 127–168.
5 Morrison, T., *Beloved*, Richmond: Alma Classics, 2017.
6 Cervantes, M., *Don Quixote I*, The Author's Preface, Canterbury Classics, Charlotte, NC: Baker & Taylor, 2013.
7 Homer, *The Iliad*, London: William Heinemann Ltd., 1924.
8 Anonymous, *The Song of Roland*, D. L. Sayers (Trans.), Important Books, 2013.
9 Sterne, L., *The Life and Opinions of Tristram Shandy, Gentleman*, New York: Norton, 1980.
10 Ross, I. C., *Laurence Sterne, A Life*, Oxford: Oxford University Press, 2001.
11 Boccaccio, G., *The Decameron*, London: Penguin Classics, 2003.
12 Scarlatti, A. (1721) *La Griselda*; Vivaldi, A. (1735) *Griselda*; Massenet, J. (1901) *Griselidis*.
13 Arendt, H., Totalitarianism, in *The Origins of Totalitarianism*, Cleveland, OH: The World Publishing Company, 1951, p. 350.
14 Freud, S., *A Project for a Scientific Psychology*, S.E. 1, London: Hogarth, pp. 281–397.

Chapter 5

Traumas in Freud's Life

"Unfortunately my father was one of these perverts"

In a letter to Fliess[1] dated September 21, 1897, Freud announces that he is abandoning the psychoanalysis of trauma that he calls his Neurotica:

> And now I want to confide in you [...] the great secret that has been slowly dawning on me in the last few months. I no longer believe in my *neurotica*.

Thus, he abandons the seduction theory he brought back from his stay in Paris in 1885 and 1886. There, aside from attending Charcot's classes at La Salpêtrière, he also attended Paul Brouardel's lectures and his autopsies at the morgue, on children who had been raped and murdered. In 1891, he portrayed the famous medical examiner in premonitory terms:

> He used to show us from post-mortem material at the morgue how much there was which deserved to be known by doctors but of which science preferred to take no notice.

Even today, when people are encouraged to speak, there is still "much" which is dismissed as "phantasy" by the perpetrators of such acts or by those who prefer not to see. Freud's grandson Clement Freud, a media personality and British Member of Parliament, was accused of paedophilia after his death in 2009, by victims who were children at the time. Was he following in the traces of his great-grandfather Jacob, which the founder of psychoanalysis had erased?

One of the reasons Freud gives for abandoning his Neurotica is that he finds the frequency of paedophilic acts reported by his patients hard to believe. He writes of his "surprise that in all cases, the father, not excluding my own, had to be accused of being perverse—[...], whereas surely such widespread perversions against children are not very probable".

DOI: 10.4324/9781003257592-7

Yet on February 8, 1897 he had confided to Fliess the likelihood of such acts in his own family. In the complete version of their correspondence, which had been censured by Anna Freud,[2] the letter bearing this date includes the unequivocal description of an instance of fellatio that produced "a hysterical headache", followed by the admission:

> Unfortunately my father was one of these perverts, and is responsible for the hysteria of my brother and those of several younger sisters. The frequency of this circumstance often makes me wonder.

Jacob Freud died on October 18, 1896. On November 2, his son related to Fliess a "nice" dream he had "the night after the funeral":

> I was in a place where I read a sign: 'You are requested to close the eyes.' I immediately recognized the place as the barbershop I visit every day.

When Freud abandoned the psychoanalysis of traumas a year later, was he complying with this injunction? Afterwards, he opened his eyes on several occasions, always in a catastrophic context. First, in 1907, after reading a short story about recovery from a delusion involving the destruction of Pompeii; in 1914, when his sons left to fight at the front; again in 1919, when his daughter Sophie died of the Spanish flu; and finally three years later her son Heinele died as well, and Freud learned he had jaw cancer. The Nazi terror brought another trauma: after the burning of his books in Berlin in 1933, under Goebbels' orders, Freud feared that psychoanalysis would not survive.

"Ashes, ashes, we all fall down". The only ones who could already see the ashes of the "final solution" were lucid grown-up children who warned of impending catastrophe, but were discredited by those around them. They are the "messengers of disaster", to quote Annette Becker's beautiful title.[3] Her book is centred on Raphael Lemkin and Jan Karski who, in 1941, "foresaw the magnitude of the destruction of the European Jews, but were met with indifference and rejection".

Dolfi, Freud's sister, a Cassandra-like old maid

In 1958, Martin, Freud's son (named Jean Martin in honour of Charcot), went against his sister Anna's advice and published a biography entitled *Sigmund Freud: Man and Father*, on the occasion of his birth centennial. From the very first chapter, Martin speaks of his aunts, including Dolfi, the youngest.

> She was not clever on in any way remarkable, and it might be true to say that constant attendance on Amalia [her mother] had suppressed her

personality into a condition of dependence from which she never recovered. Alone of my father's sisters, she did not marry. Perhaps this made her somewhat unusual and subjective to impressions, or forebodings, of coming disasters which we thought ridiculous and even a little silly.

A combination of apparent silliness and constant vigilance is characteristic of abused children, whose reclusiveness is accompanied by hyperacuity to perversion. The silly old maid gives her nephew a demonstration of this one day, when they are walking in Vienna in the 1930s:

> ... we passed an ordinary kind of man, probably a Gentile, who, so far as I knew, had taken no notice of us. I put it down to a pathological phobia, or Dolfi's stupidity, when she gripped my arm in terror and whispered: 'Did you hear what that man said? He called me a dirty stinking Jewess and said it was time we were all killed'.

Twenty years later, Martin marvels at his blindness, and that of his friends, regarding the imminent extermination of European Jews, foreseen that day by "a lovable but rather silly old maid". Speaking of the horrific end of his aunts, he concludes: "Dolfi herself died of starvation in Theresienstadt. The three other sisters were murdered in other camps, in 1942 and 1943".

At the end of 1945, their niece Anna was giving "the children from Terezin" a home in Sussex. At that time, she was living in London, in the Maresfield Gardens house where Freud had gone into exile with his closest family in May 1938, and where he died in September 1939. There, he finished writing *Moses and Monotheism*, started in Vienna after the burning of his books in 1933.

Freud said about this work, written intermittently over a period of years under the Nazi terror—Anna always carried a cyanide pill in case she should be arrested—that "it haunted him like a ghost". The book ends with a chapter on "historical truth", trampled by totalitarian systems aiming to destroy psychoanalysis. In fact, the cutting out of historical truth by a lawless agency—rather than its repression, which supposes the existence of the symbolic order—is what the analysis of madness and trauma strives to repair.

Freud's entire oeuvre is indeed haunted by his first approach, the one prior to parting ways with the Viennese physician Joseph Breuer, inventor of the "cathartic method". They had met in the 1880s and had been involved in the treatment of Bertha Pappenheim—known as Anna O—who called her therapy with Breuer a "talking cure". In 1895, Freud and Breuer published *Studies on Hysteria*[4] together. Ten years after their separation, Freud proceeds to analyse the healing of a delusion in a literary work.

Healing of a delusion

In 1907, Freud became fascinated with the subject of the novella *Gradiva: A Pompeian Fantasy*, by German writer Wilhelm Jensen, and published an essay about it: *Delusions and Dreams in Jensen's Gradiva*.[5] In this work, he recognised his psychoanalysis of traumas, that Josef Breuer went on exploring on his own. Jensen's description of the particular transference in a case of delusion tied to a historical catastrophe had the approval of the founder of psychoanalysis:

> The procedure which the author makes his Zoe adopt for curing her childhood friend's delusion shows a far-reaching similarity ... with a therapeutic method which was introduced into medical practice in 1895 by Dr. Josef Breuer and myself, and to the perfecting of which I have since then devoted myself.

Indeed, in *Studies on Hysteria*, Freud does not hesitate to admit that in such cases the transference resonates with cut-out parts of himself. He says, about patients like Miss Lucy, that they know something and do not know it at the same time. And in a footnote, he reveals an experience of his own which confirms his conviction:

> I myself have had a very remarkable experience of this sort, which is still clearly before me. [...] What happened was that I saw something which did not fit in at all with my expectations; yet I did not allow what I saw to disturb my fixed plan in the least, though the perception should have put a stop to it. I was unconscious of any contradiction in this; nor was I aware of my feelings of repulsion which must nevertheless undoubtedly have been responsible for the perception producing no psychical effect. I was afflicted by that blindness of the seeing eye which is so astonishing in the attitude of mothers to their daughters, husbands to their wives and rulers to their favourites.

... As well as the attitude of sons towards their fathers, we might add if we read between the lines. In the *Gradiva*, the cutting away does not concern a sexual scene, but rather death, as Jensen points out in a letter to Freud.[6] Referring to another of his novellas, the writer stresses that personal experience is the source of his fiction.

> The [novella] was woven from my memories, my first love for a little girl who was my close childhood friend and who died of consumption at the age of eighteen, and a young girl with whom I was friendly many years later and who was also snatched away suddenly.

The hero of the *Gradiva*, Norbert Hanold, is a young archaeologist so fascinated with the image on a bas-relief he saw in Rome that he hangs a plaster-cast of it on a wall in his office. Impressed by Jensen's story, Freud displayed the same plaster-cast replica across from his couch, as seen on the photograph of 19 Berggasse in Vienna, and in his Maresfield Gardens house in London.

The bas-relief represents a young woman whom young Norbert names Gradiva, "the woman splendid in walking". The motion of one of her feet, raised perpendicular to the ground, so fascinates him that he observes closely the ankles of all the women he passes on the street. In his delusion, he sees the young Latina girl walking in the streets of Pompeii. A terrifying dream shows her walking to the portico of a temple, where she sits down; her face "turns white as marble", just before she is buried under the ashes of Vesuvius in 79 AD.

Haunted by this ghostly being, Norbert Hanold decides to look for her in Pompeii and sets off on a journey we would call pathological today. Gradiva doesn't disappoint him. She does not fail to appear, at the archaeological site, at noon, the hour of ghosts, in the form of a real live girl. Luckily, the girl complies when he asks her to lie down, like in his dream, to be covered over by burning ashes. The young woman could have run away, called him mad, or a pervert, or not spoken to him at all. But she did.

After playing the role of the dying girl, she tells him her name: Zoe Bergang. Consumed by his delusion, Norbert had not recognised his neighbour, whose name, according to him, means "the living one who shines as she walks" ... like his Gradiva. In his own childhood, a devastating catastrophe did indeed occur, but it did not happen "to him" as Winnicott would say.[7] Very likely left totally alone at an early age after the death of both his parents, "his unlived agony is lived for the first time" in the transference to his neighbour, who went through a similar experience.

She also lost her mother, and her father, a zoologist, was more interested in the slow-worms he kept in alcohol than in his daughter. Norbert and Zoe's encounter reminds me of René Clément's film[8] *Les jeux interdits*, about "forbidden games"—in ordinary life. In the movie, a little girl, whose parents were killed in the 1940 exodus after the German invasion of France, steals crosses from cemeteries with her friend—a little boy—to place on the graves of buried animals. This play allows these children left in an abyssal time zone to perform a ritual for the dead, necessary for revival. Similarly, thanks to Zoe, whose name means "life" in Greek, the hero of the *Gradiva* can walk out the death zone—*area di morte* in the language of Gaetano Benedetti, who was an analyst of psychosis in Basel.[9]

Jensen's story allowed Freud to rediscover the time when, like Zoe, his aim was to reach a cut-out unconscious for his patients.

The unrepressed unconscious

This unconscious, which is not repressed, was the subject of British analyst Donald Winnicott's last essay, entitled "Fear of Breakdown",[10] found on his desk when he died in 1971. In it, Winnicott discusses an ever-imminent catastrophe, described as follows:

> ... the breakdown has already happened, near the beginning of the individual's life. The patient needs to 'remember' but it is not possible to remember something that has not yet happened, and this thing of the past has not happened yet because he was not there for it to happen to [there was no otherness]. The only way is to experience this past thing for the first time in the present, that is to say, in the transference.

"In this situation, the original agony can be experienced in the present by finding in the analyst's errors and failings details of the unlived past. Here, the unconscious is not exactly the repressed unconscious, nor Jung's collective unconscious".

But this unconscious has kept young Norbert in fear of breakdown, hanging on to the image of the ankle of his Gradiva, on the edge of her own catastrophe. In this regard, Freud observes in his essay: "Everything that is repressed must remain unconscious, but [...] the repressed does not comprise the whole unconscious".

In such a case, the term "return of the repressed" is inaccurate. Emmanuelle said of a patient just emerging from a coma, whose mood would change suddenly: "It was him and not him".

An unconscious that is not repressed is at the heart of madness and trauma. It resists traditional transference since it is cut out of speech, manifesting through "surviving images", or "*nachleben*" as they were called by Renaissance historian Aby Warburg, whom I mentioned earlier.

Aby Warburg: images that survive disaster

Aby Warburg's madness bursts out at the start of the Great War when, in true Quixotic style, he takes himself to be the Commander-in-chief of the German military. In his library, where a map of the warfront is displayed, he tracks the advance of the different armies, based on numerous newspaper clippings brought by his wife and children. He said, of this period, that he was flooded with sensory images recorded in his childhood, the time of the Franco-Prussian War of 1870, and the rise of mass anti-Semitism, according to Hannah Arendt. After the war, the swift French indemnity payments caused a stock market boom, followed in 1873 by a crash blamed on Jewish bankers, among whom the Director of the Warburg bank in Hamburg, Aby's father.

In 1879, at the age of 13, Aby concluded a pact with his younger brothers, giving up his right to head the family bank in exchange for being supplied with books, which his brothers in fact provided until his death. The same year, an Anti-Semitic League was founded in Hamburg by the anarchist Wilhelm Marr.[11] Aby's brothers persisted in keeping their promise, and the surviving image of the deathly threat hanging over the Jews persisted as well, until its "final" enactment in the Second World War. Hospitalised between 1921 and 1924 in Ludwig Binswanger's clinic—Freud's disciple—Aby kept howling "like an animal, that all his relatives would be deported and exterminated".[12] In 1923, Hitler was writing *Mein Kampf* in prison.

Towards the end of 1921, in an exchange of letters with Freud, Binswanger's assessment was: "I do not believe that *statu quo ante* recovery [...] is possible, any more than a return to his scientific activities". But the art historian proved them wrong. Since he kept shouting that he was in hell at the clinic, Binswanger challenged him, without much conviction, to give a lecture and prove his mind was sound. Aby gathered up his courage and, with superhuman effort, delivered his now famous *Lecture on Serpent Ritual* among Hopi Amerindians,[13] before the staff and patients in 1923.

In my opinion, Aby's good fortune consisted in the unfaltering presence of a therapist worthy of the name. His student Fritz Saxl visited him regularly, and believed his research to be as valuable by means of his madness. Born in Vienna, Saxl had just been demobilised after the war. He had probably been prepared for his master's fits of violence by witnessing psychological trauma in his army buddies. A year after the lecture, Binswanger discharged his patient and Aby Warburg continued his research until his death in 1929.

Dolfi, in her "silliness", and Aby in his madness were announcing on the front lines the catastrophe no one wanted to see coming. The sensory memory of "the body that keeps the score"[14] plays a decisive role in their prescience, promptly dismissed, to be replaced by a definitive diagnosis of deficiency.

Notes

1 Masson, J. M. (Ed.), *The Complete Letters of Sigmund Freud to Wilhelm Fliess, 1887–1904*, Cambridge, MA: Harvard University Press, 1985.
2 Masson, J. M. (Ed.), *The Complete Letters of Sigmund Freud to Wilhelm Fliess*, op. cit.
3 Becker, A., *Les Messagers du désastre. Raphael Lemkin, Jan Karski et les génocides*, Paris: Fayard, 2018.
4 Freud, S. and Breuer, J., *Studies on Hysteria*, S.E. 2, London: Hogarth, 1895.
5 Freud, S., *Delusions and Dreams in Jensen's Gradiva*, S.E. 9, London: Hogarth, 1907.

6 Freud, S., *Delusions and Dreams in Jensen's Gradiva*, op. cit. Jensen, W. letter, December 14, 1907.

7 Winnicott, D. (1974). Fear of Breakdown, in *International Review of Psycho-Analysis* 1(1–2).

8 Clement, R., *Jeux interdits*, film, 1952.

9 Benedetti, G., *The Psychotherapy of Schizophrenia*, New York: New York University, 1987.

10 Winnicott, D. W. (1974). Fear of Breakdown, in *International Review of Psycho-Analysis* 1(1–2).

11 Chernow, W., *The Warburgs*, New York: Vintage Books, 1994.

12 Koerner, J. L. (2012). Writing Rituals: The Case of Aby Warburg, in *Common Knowledge* 18(1): 86–105, Duke University Press.

13 Binswanger, L. and Warburg, A., *La Guérison infinie*, D. Stimili (Ed.), Paris: Rivages, 2007.

14 Van der Kolk, B., *The Body Keeps the Score*, New York: Penguin Books, 2014.

Chapter 6

Writers, "Our Most Valuable Allies" in Wars and Pandemics

Is it possible that for Freud the text of the *Gradiva* played the role of a surviving image after he abandoned his Neurotica, as might be surmised by the fact that he placed the plaster cast of the Gradiva across from the couch in his consulting room?

The eruption of the Vesuvius appropriately describes the critical sessions in which a "timequake" takes place in the midst of the periods of "stagnation" Emmanuelle mentioned. "I'm tired of Covid!" she said, when she kept having to start over again. Freud experienced the same discouragement, that he confessed to Fliess in a letter dated September 21, 1897: "The continual disappointment [...]; the running away of patients who for a period of time had been most gripped [by analysis]; the absence of the complete success on which I had counted...".

I am borrowing the term "timequake" from the title of Kurt Vonnegut's last book,[1] which was the topic of Jean-Max Gaudillière's last seminar.[2] The American author asserts that the writing of this book completes the telling of his war experience and of his captivity in the cellar of a Dresden slaughterhouse, during the bombardment that destroyed the city in February 1945. Having started this narration in *Slaughterhouse-Five*, published in 1969 and immediately crowned with critical acclaim, Vonnegut was able to finish it 20 years later, after he discovered, when giving a lecture in Rochester, the grave of the buddy portrayed in his bestseller by the hero, Billy Pilgrim. Until then, Vonnegut had believed him to have been buried in Dresden, without funeral rites, in a paper suit, and had never revealed his name.[3]

A similar encounter occurred for Freud when he read Jensen's novella. He came face to face with the psychoanalysis of trauma he had abandoned, as he read about the transference between Norbert, the delusional hero, and Zoe. Norbert doesn't recognise his childhood friend because for him she emerges from a different temporal sphere. After the two characters carry out a funeral rite on a quasi mythological stage for the dead who haunt them both, time can resume its flow. Similarly, Freud can take up the thread of his first research interests, which he thought he had left behind. Thus, at the beginning of his essay on the *Gradiva*, he writes:

DOI: 10.4324/9781003257592-8

... creative writers are valuable allies— Freud calls them *bundesgenos-sen,* travelling companions[4] —, and their evidence is to be prized highly, for they are apt to know a whole host of things between heaven and earth of which our philosophy has not yet let us dream. In their knowledge of the mind they are far in advance of us everyday people, for they draw upon sources which we have not yet opened up for science.

Indeed, the writers discussed in our seminars were our travelling companions—as was Boccacio for me recently—on the arduous path of madness and trauma, for they do in fact know a host of things of which our Schools remain ignorant.

The role of the historical truth

The Great War and its aftermath affected Freud deeply, as Max Schur, his personal physician,[5] testifies. He had no news of his two sons fighting at the front. Due to a lack of patients, his financial situation deteriorated drastically. In 1920, he lost his daughter Sophie, his "ray of sunshine" to the Spanish flu pandemic. In 1923, Sophie's youngest child, Heinele, Freud's favourite grandson, died of tuberculous meningitis at the age of four and a half. The same year, diagnosed with cancer of the jaw, Freud underwent repeated surgeries and was fitted with prostheses that inflicted much pain, interfering with his ability to eat and to speak in public. This explains his severe expression on photographs of this period, an expression, sad to say, imitated by today's dead serious analysts.

Wartime and the influenza epidemic reactivated Freud's reflection on an unconscious that is not "structured like a language", as Lacan says, but produces surviving images from a past disaster. *The Uncanny,*[6] published in 1919, repeats the statement made in the *Gradiva,* about a non-repressed unconscious: "... this last way of putting it no doubt strains the term 'repression' beyond its legitimate meaning".

The same remark could have applied in 1920, in *Beyond the Pleasure Principle,* to the nightmares of soldiers suffering from traumatic neuroses, and over ten years later to Freud himself, when this unconscious drove him to write under the Nazi terror, after Hitler came to power in January 1933. Between the burning of Freud's books on Babelplatz in Berlin on May 12 of the same year and his precipitated departure from Vienna five years later, he began to write *Moses and Monotheism,* taking it up repeatedly, since this text "haunted [him] like an unlaid ghost".

What haunted him is stated after he reached London in 1938, in the last part of the book entitled "The Historical Truth", in which he remarks that delusion, *Wahn,* contains a kernel of truth. Freud's *Preliminary Remark* to this text—dated March 1938 and written just before he left Vienna—testifies to the mortal danger he faced by dealing with that subject:

> So I shall not publish this essay. But that need not hinder me from writing it. [...] Thus it may lie hid until the time comes when it may safely venture into the light of day, or until someone else who reaches the same opinions and conclusions can be told: 'In darker days there lived a man who thought as you did'.

His conclusions do not apply to the entire body of his already published work, but rather to the historical truth and to its witnesses, assassinated by the totalitarian systems he cites in the same *Preliminary Remark*:

> We find with astonishment that progress has concluded an alliance with barbarism. In Soviet Russia the attempt has been made to better the life of a hundred million people till now held in oppression. [But] the authorities [...] robbed them of every possibility of freedom of thought.

The "someone else" Freud wishes for in these dark times could be the philosopher Ludwig Wittgenstein, whose Preface to the *Philosophical Investigations*,[7] written in 1945, faithfully echoes Freud's own thoughts:

> I make my remarks public with doubtful feelings. It is not impossible that it should fall to the lot of this work, in its poverty and in the darkness of this time, to bring light into one brain or another—but, of course, it is not likely. I should have liked to produce a good book. This has not come about, but the time is past in which I could improve it.

We shall see that despite his criticism of psychoanalysis, Wittgenstein is our "valuable ally" who contends that there is transference when there seems to be none, since "the tool with the name is broken".

The absence of funeral rites at the height of the pandemic is a poignant illustration of this. Anne Lise finds it "atrocious" for families is not to see their loved ones after their death. Jessica obtained permission for the children to say good-bye to their deceased mother. According to historian Stéphane Audoin-Rouzeau,[8] not to accompany the dying constitutes a major anthropological transgression, something which profoundly affects the social body.

This "something", although quickly erased by a return to normalcy, bursts through in delusions and traumatic revivals, which carry "a fragment of historical truth". The term "political subject" to designate the emergence in transference of what took place in the social body occurred to me when I read *The Political Self*, with an Introduction and a chapter by Rod Tweedy,[9] former editor at Karnac.

Notes

1 Vonnegut, K., *Timequake*, Westminster: Penguin Books, 1997.
2 Gaudillière, J.-M., *The Birth of a Political Self. Seminars 2001–2014*, London: Routledge, 2021.
3 Schields, C., *And So It Goes, Kurt Vonnegut, a Life*, New York: Henry Holt and Company, 2011.
4 I thank Jeanna Wolf Bernstein, psychoanalyst in Vienna, for this translation.
5 Schur, M., *Freud: Living and Dying*, New York: International Universities Press, 1972.
6 Freud, S., *The Uncanny*, S.E. 17, London: Hogarth, 1919.
7 Wittgenstein, L. (1953). *Philosophical Investigations*, Oxford: Oxford University Press, 1983.
8 Audoin-Rouzeau, S., article "Nous ne reverrons jamais le monde que nous avons quitté il y a un mois (We will never go back to the world we left a month ago)", on Mediapart, April 12, 2030.
9 Tweedy, R. (Ed.), *A Political Self*, London: Karnac Books, 2017.

Chapter 7

A Political Subject

"My delusion emerges at the crossroads of my story with world history".

These words were spoken as an introduction by a young philosopher who had run away from the clinic where his analyst had prescribed electroshock to suppress his "delusional masterpiece". I owe this expression to Gaetano Benedetti, whom we visited every year in Basel at Carnival time. He told us he was against the therapeutic use of electric current, preferring the current which passed between him and his patients.

Like Norbert Hanold, this young man had lost his wits while visiting the Capitol in Rome, where he proclaimed he was the Emperor. When I stepped into his delusion, inadvertently, as Winnicott says, arrested time was set in motion again. His mother had died shortly after the war, during which his father had been on good terms with German businessmen.

I have often told the story of this crucial session where a "timequake" occurred.[1] One morning, he told me: "You look washed out today". Touched to the quick, I protested that I was in great shape, and he took his leave. Once he left, I realised that this was the day when I was expecting test results, to find out if I had cancer. Later, relieved that the results were negative, I called him to say that he had been right.

When he came back, he explained that he had noticed in me the same fatigue which embarrassed him as a child when his mother, suffering from cancer, took him to school. Up until then, he had believed his childhood to have been happy; he had not even been taken to his mother's funeral. Now, the shame that befell the family during the Purge—which, as an episode in French history started after May 1945—was finally brought to light.

Things speak when people are silent

After the war, we carry on; analysts build new theories and, like everyone else, often set aside what has just taken place.

Thomas Kohut, a modern German historian, son of psychoanalyst Heinz Kohut[2] who emigrated from Vienna to America in 1939, told us how, as a child, he would hear the Yiddish accent in his father's discussions with

DOI: 10.4324/9781003257592-9

his colleagues about new concepts, but never heard them mention the time before their emigration. But in the street, when his father saw a hole dug by workers, he would make a wide detour just in case a bomb might explode, you never know!

Here in Europe, in his opening address on "psychic causality"[3] at the Bonneval Conference on September 28, 1946, Lacan made no mention of the war except briefly, to justify the abandoning of his practice during the war years.

Yet there were analysts who worked on the front lines during the two world wars, with traumatised soldiers and civilians. Child analyst Françoise Dolto continued to see children like Léon, a Jewish little boy who was unable to hold himself up because he was attached to a chair all day in his parents' clandestine workshop.[4] Herself a war child of the previous war, Dolto spoke to the chair which had become one with the boy, and had helped to shield the family from the terror of arrest. Once the vital function of the chair was recognised, little Léon was able to stand and walk.

Manon Pignot's book *Allons enfants de la patrie*[5] reveals that Françoise Dolto was already a therapist at the age of 6, in the letters she sent her beloved godfather, who was fighting in the alpine troops on the front lines. When he was killed in 1915, she declared herself a widow, just like the women she saw becoming distraught at the announcement of the death of their husbands or sons.

The idea of talking to a chair is not so strange, when as a child you heard stories where things and animals speak when humans are unable to do so. The young heroine of *Baba Yaga*[6] escapes from the terrible witch by speaking to a flower she frees from the design of her needlework, to the dogs and the cat, to the gate that creaks and to the birch tree, helping them all.

Stories, nursery rhymes and songs perpetuate the therapeutic art of storytelling, as we saw in the *Decameron*. The proverbs of Madagascar serve the same purpose. Jean Paulhan,[7] author of the little book *L'expérience du proverbe* I mentioned to Nanosy, describes Malagasy proverbs as "little dramas or fables to resolve a dispute or close a discussion". Paulhan contends that the storyteller must involve his body, to physically transmit the power of the images when mere words are not enough. *Don Quixote* abounds with Sancho's proverbs, as well as songs set to music by Jordi Savall,[8] who plays his viola de gamba, to let us hear the music of the novel familiar to Cervantes's contemporaries.

Our profession is also rooted in the oral tradition and I make use of this spontaneously since, as a child, I often heard adults emphasise certain situations by singing the beginning of a song or the first lines of a poem. Sometimes, in a session, a song comes to my mind, that echoes what I am being told, and during our seminars, I would start to hum some popular tune which the participants sang in a happy chorus. Jean Paulhan points out the joy that springs from overcoming the effort of putting things into words:

If we had to explain this clumsiness, we would have to say that certain words must be taken for things. They are particular things that it is urgent to say, and to say as exactly as possible — so that, in regard to these things, or these words, a whole portion of language serves to establish that it is possible to speak.

At the start of our exchanges by video, Lucie, Jessica and Franck spoke of joy, contrasting with depressing discourses. In these situations, like in my practice, "a whole portion of language serves to establish that it is possible to speak". The task is not easy when the given word has lost its value and symptoms appear only to be interpreted as mental illness.

Bessel Van der Kolk: the body keeps the score[9]

In his recent book, Bessel Van der Kolk shows that in instances of trauma, there is a neuronal disconnection of the prefrontal hemisphere, which gives access to the symbolic dimension of words and to the sense of time. When confronting danger, the animal brain takes over to keep us alive, triggering reactions of flight, aggression, simulated death or submission. These modes of survival are physically recorded, outside the realm of speech and of time, in the form of sensory images which resurface at the least sign of danger.

The author dedicated the book to his patients who, by retaining the mark of traumatic events, became "textbooks" for their therapist. The word "score" in Kolk's title can also refer to musical notation. By deciphering the score together, his patients taught him that so-called psychotic symptoms: voices, visions, delusions or refusal to communicate, convey information about traumas endured in "another time". Diagnosed as "dissociation", they are considered symptoms of pathology, while in truth they save your life. This was the conclusion reached by Van der Kolk after years of research.

In 1978, while he was a young psychiatrist in a Boston hospital for veterans of the Vietnam war, he was helpless to treat their rage or their withdrawal. To understand what was going on in their brains, he turned to neurology and began to get some answers in the 1990s, thanks to the invention of brain imaging.

In 1999, when a couple who barely escaped being killed in a pileup on the highway arrived uninjured at a Boston hospital, Van der Kolk asked them to consent to a brain scan. It revealed a neuronal disconnection between the neocortex and the limbic system common to all mammals. To disqualify this expertise by seeing it simply as a primitive animal reaction would truly be human stupidity.

The therapy consists of addressing those dissociated parts by letting them speak: literally, *logon didonai*—giving speech and reason, where the *logos* was interrupted. By doing so, the therapist shows that this experience is not foreign to him. In contrast, mainstream analytic techniques fail to reach these parts of the psyche, at once present and unattainable, for which the other does not exist. Only the alliance of two people sharing the experience in the present can reach these cut-out parts, by acknowledging that the dissociation occurred *with reason* and that surviving in absolute solitude takes great courage. Then, little by little, the terrified child or adult lets down his guard and intense images start to be interwoven in the "language game"—a term coined by Wittgenstein—of transference.

***

Bessel Ban der Kolk was born in Holland in 1944 and almost died of malnutrition in the 1944–1945 famine in that country. He recounts this in his conversation with Cathy Caruth[10] for her book *Listening to Trauma*, in which his contemporary in Amsterdam, Onno van der Hart, describes his work with trauma-related dissociation. This approach was used by Dutch psychotherapists who treated deportees returning from concentration camps, as I learned from one of their descendants. On this other front line of the battle with the unnamable, they discovered that the symptoms of dissociation were what allowed these prisoners to survive.

I would have liked it if some of these therapists could have been at the Lutetia Hotel when the deportees came back. My father went right past his brother Émile without recognising him, until the latter called out to him. A member of the mountain infantry, Émile had fought in the battle of Narvik in 1940, had joined the Resistance when he returned, and was deported, probably to Mauthausen—we can't be sure because he never talked about it. But he gave his brother a book entitled *The Tunnel*,[11] saying: "Here, if you want to know…". It is a story about the prisoners of this camp and the tunnel they constructed in the Loibl Pass between Austria and Yugoslavia (present-day Slovenia). When he returned from the war, Émile sent back all his decorations.

If he had met one of the Dutch therapists, the man cut off from our world could have emerged as a "political self"[12]—to use Rod Tweedy's term—insisting on showing what cannot be said, at the crossroads of History with personal history, as Dolfi did in her "silliness", as well as Aby Warburg and the young philosopher in their delusions. Ending the dissociation was the aim of two philosophers who had fought wars.

***

Wittgenstein: what cannot be said cannot stay silent

Ludwig Wittgenstein wrote his *Tractatus Philosophicus* while fighting on the Eastern front in the Austrian army. This treatise, published in 1921, ended with the statement: "Whereof one cannot speak, thereof one must remain silent". But he would later change his assertion, to go beyond this silence, as we can read in the Preface to the 1946 edition[13] of the *Investigations*:

Four years ago I had occasion to re-read my first book (the *Tractatus Logico-Philosophicus*) and to explain its ideas to someone. It suddenly seemed to me that I should publish those old thoughts and the new ones together: that the latter could be seen in the right light only by contrast with and against the background of my old way of thinking. For since beginning to occupy myself with philosophy again, sixteen years ago, I have been forced to recognize grave mistakes in what I wrote in that first book.

Indeed, in the *Investigations* the philosopher's perspective has undergone a radical change: what cannot be said cannot help but be shown through an "ostensive definition". But shown to whom?

Sixteen years earlier, in 1929, Wittgenstein found a place where he could address the insistent symptoms of his silence. He returned to Cambridge at the invitation of the young philosopher Georges Moore, with whom he had attended Bertrand Russel's courses before the war. Having left Austria for good, he took up his philosophy, abandoned in Vienna for ten years after his return from the front and from his year-long captivity in Monte Cassino.[14]

Like Apollinaire who returned to Paris in 1916 with a head wound, he did not take off his old uniform; but, unlike the poet, he stopped writing, overwhelmed by posttraumatic wounds. He became a village teacher in Upper Austria, hit his pupils, was prosecuted in 1926, and found refuge in a convent where he worked a few months as a gardener. To help him, his sister Gretl Stonborough, who had been Freud's patient for two years, suggested that he participate in the design and construction of her house, with disciples of the architect Adolf Loos. Today, the Wittgenstein House in Vienna is open to visitors.

Three years later, when he returned to Cambridge, he formulated his "second philosophy" as a form of therapy, if we believe § 133 of the *Investigations*: "There is not a single philosophical method, though there are indeed methods, like different therapies". Why not take this statement at face value, given that Descartes himself ties his philosophical method to the traumatic dreams which frightened him while he served as a soldier in the Thirty Years War.

Descartes as psychotherapist

In his *Discourse on Method* published in 1637, Descartes locates the origin of "his" method in the period of time he spent in Germany—between 1619 and 1621—where he had been called "by the wars that are not yet ended there". The Thirty Years' War started in May 1618 and ended in May 1648. "As I was returning to the army from the coronation of the Emperor, the setting in of winter arrested me in a locality where [...] I remained the whole day in [a stove-heated room] with full opportunity to occupy my attention with my own thoughts". The date is November 10, 1619, St. Martin's Eve. The young soldier's sleep is invaded by nightmares, but the dawn finds him filled with enthusiasm.[15]

He had enlisted in 1618, at 22,—"moved by a temporary heating of the liver which inspired a passion for arms"[16]—as a volunteer in the Protestant troops of Prince Maurice of Orange, at Breda. A talented fencer, he wrote a treatise—since lost, on the Art of fencing. In Breda, by chance, Descartes met the scientist Isaac Beeckman on the street, standing before a mathematical problem posted on a wall. The young soldier bragged that he could solve the problem and he proceeded to do so. This was the start of a friendship that rekindled Descartes' passion for the sciences.

His biographer, Adrien Baillet,[17] portrays him as determined to join the Catholic troops of the Duke of Bavaria, who were fighting the Protestant Frederick V, recently enthroned King of Bohemia. When he left Holland, still as a volunteer without mercenary status or political beliefs—asserting: "I was not concerned to follow the convictions of States or Princes whose subject I did not happen to be by birth"—he crossed several countries and stopped in Frankfurt, where Ferdinand II, the Catholic pretender to the throne of Bohemia, was crowned emperor on August 28, 1619. Then he took up solitary residence during winter quarters near Neuburg on the Danube, in Northern Bavaria.

It was there, in his stove-heated room, that he had the three dreams[18] recounted by Baillet. In the first dream, he was pursued by ghosts and battered by violent winds that made him fear he could be knocked down at every step. On waking from the second dream, "he felt a real pain, which made him fear that this might have been the work of some evil genius who wished to seduce him". He fell asleep again, only to be awakened by a deafening clap of thunder and, to his great dismay, see his bedroom full of sparks of light. Will-o'-the-wisps are said to be manifestations of the souls of the dead.

The third dream, "which was not frightening like the first two", was decisive — Descartes declared—for the discovery "of the foundations of an admirable science" In the dream, books are spread before him, including a Dictionary *and* a poetry anthology. On wakening, he decides to continue his research while travelling, guided by

> the power of imagination which enables the seeds of wisdom (existing in the minds of all men as do sparks of fire in flint) to sprout with much more facility and even much more brilliance than Reason can do in Philosophers.

However, as the biographer informs us, two more years passed before Descartes could carry out his knight errant project. One year later, he joined the troops of the Duke of Bavaria which were advancing towards Prague, and he probably fought in the Battle of White Mountain on November 9, 1620. The victory of the Catholic armies caused King Frederick, the "Winter King", to flee. His daughter Elizabeth came to know Descartes, as we shall see. In March 1621, he left the Duke's forces to join Count of Bucquoy's troops, crossed into Hungary from Bohemia, "took part in several sieges" and apparently distinguished himself. But the lifting of the siege of Neuhausel, a setback for the Imperial army, added to the loss of his General—Bucquoy was killed during the siege, in July 1621—finally turned him away from the profession of arms. Consequently, he undertook to travel, "impelled by the desire to know other countries and other customs".

Eighteen years later, while living in Holland, Descartes wrote his *Discourse* to understand what happened to him, and to apply his method to the traumatic dreams that perhaps continued to haunt him, since he makes use of the terms he employed to describe them: "like a man walking alone in the dark, I resolve to proceed slowly and with such circumspection, that if I do not advance far, I will at least guard against falling".

Knowing that it was still wartime when Descartes was composing the *Discourse*, it might be supposed that the philosopher was analysing the need to dissociate "animal spirits" from thought.

Once this was done, he acted as a psychotherapist to the young Princess Elisabeth of Bohemia, whom he met in The Hague (La Haye) in 1642. Coincidentally, La Haye-en-Touraine was the name of the town where Descartes was born in 1596; it has now been renamed "Descartes". The princess and the philosopher exchanged letters between 1643 and 1649, when Descartes left for Stockholm, at the invitation of Christina, Queen of Sweden. Descartes died there six weeks after his arrival.

In her letters, Elisabeth complains of psychosomatic symptoms and is critical of Cartesian dualism. Descartes answers that after having at first dissociated the body and the soul, he must now reunite them. He speaks of disturbances arising from his own childhood. Indeed, he had believed that his mother died giving birth to him, when in fact she died a year later, after giving birth to a baby who did not survive.

The transference creating a bond between the two of them was resonating at the crossroads of their personal histories with History. Elisabeth was the daughter of the king of Bohemia, Frederick V, the "Winter King", who was deposed in 1620 after the defeat at White Mountain, near Prague. The princess lived all her life in exile, since the day her father was banished from Prague in 1621, when she was a baby. Her "philosophical love affair" with Descartes—to quote the title of Yaelle Malpertu's book,[19]—was no doubt therapeutic. In Wittgenstein's case, many years had to pass before he could elaborate his philosophy "as a therapy".

Wittgenstein's method

The method is defined in paragraph 41 of the *Philosophical Investigations*[20]:

> Now suppose that the tool with the name "N" is broken. [...] Here one might say: "N" has become meaningless; and this [...] would mean that sign "N" no longer had a use in our language, and the one to whom the sign is addressed is lost.

Instead of keeping silent or interpreting this loss of meaning as mental illness, the philosopher offers another solution:

> But we could also imagine a convention whereby B has to shake his head in reply if A gives him the sign belonging to a tool that is broken. — In this way the command "N" might be said to be given a place in the language-game even when the tool no longer exists, and the sign "N" to have meaning even when its bearer ceases to exist.

This nod of the head means *"touché"*. The diaries kept by Nanosy, the daily phone calls Lucie and Jessica made to patients' families, even if they only said a few words, are an equivalent to this. In the silence at the other end, the breath heard in response is perceived as an answering sign of agreement, taking its "place in a language-game", when "the tool with the words is broken".

The year of the *Anschluss*, Wittgenstein applies this method to himself. In 1938, all structures ensuring reliability collapse in his native Austria. He then travels to Dublin, to stay with his disciple Maurice O'Connor Drury,[21] whom he had advised to study medicine rather than philosophy. Ludwig asks his friend to take him to the psychiatric hospital. He wishes to speak to patients condemned to live behind a wall of silence, whom no one visits. Drury recounts that his recurrent visits were greatly appreciated by these men, particularly one of them, whom Wittgenstein judged to be "more intelligent than his doctors". A language game was set in motion again for both him and these patients.

The philosopher, like the professionals I interviewed, played the double role of the *therapon*, as described in *The Iliad*: "second in combat" in the war against that which destroys the bond of speech, and "ritual double" in charge of funeral rites, when they are impossible to provide, like in times of war and pandemics.

Notes

1   Davoine, F. and Gaudillière, J.-M., *History beyond Trauma*, New York: Other Press, 2004.
2   Kohut, H., *The Analysis of the Self. Psychoanalytic Treatment of Narcissistic Personality Disorders*, Chicago, IL: University of Chicago Press, 1971.

3 Lacan, J., Remarks on Psychic Causality, in Le *Problème de la psychogenèse des névroses et des psychoses*, H. Ey, (Ed.), Paris: Desclée de Brouwer, 1950, and in *Écrits*, Paris: Seuil, 1966.
4 Dolto, F., *L'Image inconsciente du corps* (The Unconscious Image of the Body), Paris: Seuil, 1984.
5 Pignot, M., *Allons enfants de la patrie*, Paris: Seuil, 2012.
6 Wiginton, J., *Baba Yaga Tales*, Scotts Valley, CA: CreateSpace Publishing, 2018.
7 Paulhan, J., *L'expérience du proverbe*, op. cit.
8 Savall, J., *Don Quijote de la Mancha – Romances y Musicas*, CD, Alia Vox, Spain, 2006.
9 Van der Kolk, B., *The Body Keeps the Score*, op. cit.
10 Caruth, C., *Listening to Trauma: Conversations with the Leaders in the Theory & Treatment of Catastrophic Experience*, Baltimore, MD: Johns Hopkins University Press, 2014.
11 Lacaze, A., *The Tunnel*, B. W. Dower (Trans.), London: Penguin Books, 1978.
12 Tweedy, R., *The Political Self*, op. cit.
13 Wittgenstein, L., *Philosophical Investigations*, G. E. M. Anscombe (Trans.), London: Basil Blackwell, 1958.
14 Monk R., *Ludwig Wittgenstein: The Duty of Genius*, London: Penguin Books, 1990.
15 Baillet, A. (1691). *La Vie de Monsieur Descartes*, Paris: La Table ronde, 1946.
16 Haldane, E. S., *DESCARTES His Life and Times*, London: John Murray, 1905.
17 Baillet, A., *La Vie de Monsieur Descartes*, op. cit.
18 Descartes, R., Olympica, in *Vie de Monsieur Descartes*, op. cit.; *Discourse on Method and Meditations*, New York: Dover Philosophical Classics, 2003; *The Correspondence between Princess Elisabeth of Bohemia and René Descartes*, Chicago, IL: University of Chicago Press, 2007.
19 Malpertu, Y., *Une liaison philosophique. Du thérapeutique entre Descartes et la princesse Elizabeth de Bohême*, Paris: Stock, 2012.
20 Wittgenstein, L., *Philosophical Investigations*, op. cit.
21 Drury, M. O'C., Conversations with Wittgenstein, in *Ludwig Wittgenstein. Personal Recollections*, R. Rhees (Ed.), Oxford: Blackwell Publishing, 1981.

Chapter 8

Man Is a Ceremonial Animal

Death in Wittgenstein's life

Ludwig's three older brothers committed suicide: Hans and Rudi before the war, and Kurt in front of his troops on the Italian front, on Armistice Day. His surviving older brother, Paul, a gifted pianist, was taken prisoner in Russia and lost his right arm. It was for him that Ravel composed the Piano Concerto for the Left Hand, in 1930. That year, Ludwig read anthropologist Frazer's book,[1] and observed in his *Remarks on Frazer's Golden Bough*[2]:

> A whole mythology is deposited in our language. Casting out death and slaying death; but on the other hand he is also represented as a skeleton, as if he were in some sense dead himself.

In that case, Wittgenstein contends, it is always possible to invent a ritual. "Go ahead, now is the time", Jessica tells the families who pray for them. According to the philosopher:

> One could very easily invent primitive practices oneself, using the association of ideas model. One could [then] speak of the association of practices. [...] One could almost say that man is a ceremonial animal.

We discovered such an association of practices when we visited the Sioux of South Dakota, who call themselves the Lakota, a tribe of Native American warriors we only knew about from Western movies.

Giveaway

At the end of 1979, we were invited to speak about Lacan at the Austen Riggs Center, a clinic dedicated to the psychoanalysis of psychoses, where we returned the following summer. It is then that we met psychologist Jerry Mohatt[3] who came from the Rosebud Reservation in South Dakota, where he had a ranch. With the Lakota people, he had founded the Sinte Gleska

DOI: 10.4324/9781003257592-10

University, where their history, language and traditions were taught. When he heard us speak of *potlatch* in a talk in which we quoted Lacan's seminar *The Ethics of Psychoanalysis*,[4] he said: "Your topic reminds me of what the medicine men say. Come and visit me".

The day after our arrival in Pierre, the capital of South Dakota, Jerry drove us to the banks of the Missouri River, where we joined a gathering for a *Giveaway* ritual. This is where my "association of practices" comes in.

In the middle of a large circle around which we were the only two Pale-faces, there lay an enormous pile of objects, in front of which an old woman sat in her armchair, with her family standing beside her. Men forming a circle around a large drum were chanting in deep, guttural tones, setting the rhythm for dancers wearing feather headdresses and traditional costumes.

When the music stopped, all the objects were given away to those who were present, including us, and dollar bills were distributed by the old woman to the dancers who had come from afar.

While we were invited to share a meal in the tipi of a friend of Jerry' who wore a long-feathered headdress, we were asked about the origin of their French family names: Beauvais, Roubidou, Toulouse and many others. They told us that they had received them from French *coureurs des bois*, who had named their people the "Sioux". They also explained the ritual we had just seen. The family in the middle of the circle had lost several of its members in a car accident, and had waited two years to accumulate enough goods and money so that they could give everything away at the *Giveaway*, where this voluntary loss would reanimate desire, with the breath of life revived by the rhythm of the chants and the dances.

This suggested to me "an association of practices"—admittedly a bit far-fetched. Indeed, when I am running out of resources and the patient thinks of ending the sessions, I often give away a story taken from my favourite books or even from some lived experience. "At such moments", said the young philosopher referring to his delusional state on the Capitol, "I feel as if I enter a dance or a script that I know nothing about but in which I play my role perfectly". My *giveaway* of a little story may start to weave a minimal social link.

For the Intensive Care doctors and nurses I interviewed, the unexpected gift of words they received in times of distress from the families of patients in critical care was a source of energy.

Mitakuye oyasin, all my relatives

Back on the Reservation—where we returned several summers in a row—another association of practices came to my mind, during ceremonies conducted by medicine man Joe Eagle Elk. He knelt in the middle of a circle, before a little mound of earth on which ribbons of various colours were intertwined as well as a chain of little balls of red tissue, each one containing a pinch of tobacco. These had been made by the person sitting near him, who had made them while thinking about his request for the ceremony. Joe's chant in Lakota called the spirits, his allies, and described the vision that had impelled him to become a medicine man. After this initial gift of words, the one who asked for the ceremony made his request, often on behalf of a family member besieged by illness or misfortune.

Seated in a circle, a sprig of sage behind our ear, we drew a puff on the pipe being passed around, saying: "all my relatives". Each person told a personal story that came to mind, short or long, ending it with the ritual phrase "all those to whom I am related": not only humans, whom they place on the lowest level of living beings, but also animals, plants and rocks, who do not need Man to survive. If someone had nothing to say, as was the case with me in that intimidating situation, it was enough to say "all my relatives" and the next person could start speaking. "*Mitakuye oyasin*" is the only phrase I know in Lakota, so often have I heard it. After everyone had spoken, the medicine man delivered his message to the one who requested the ritual.

Then, lights came on in the room, because ceremonies are held in the dark since the still recent era when their rituals were forbidden. A joyful feast began, during which "the patient" treated everyone to boiled meat, "fry bread", and *wojapi*, stewed chalk cherries. Laughter sprang up and jokes in Rabelaisian style brought us back to earth. This had been the role the satirical comedies played between Greek tragedies, or the farces called "Kyogen" in Japanese Noh theatre.

In our meetings with Joe Eagle Elk, we discussed associated practices. We told each other clinical stories, as we did with our colleagues at Austen Riggs, and as I did with the professionals I interviewed for this book. Our common focus was to "draw out" patients—the verb used by the Intensive Care workers—from their isolation, and bring them into the circle of those to whom they are related.

Vision quest: searching for a vision

Sensory images that survive a disaster are the foundation of another ritual, the "Vision Quest". Instead of being dreaded and considered a pathology, visions are actively sought. After guidance from a medicine man during a long period of preparation, the young vision seeker climbs to the top of a hill naked, enveloped in a patchwork quilt decorated with a star. He stays there two or three days, waiting for the vision or for voices that will—or will not— manifest themselves. When he comes down from the hill, he has a series of talks with the medicine man, during which the images he has seen or sounds he has heard intertwine with the words spoken between them.

"When you see something, don't be frozen into silence; you must talk to the vision", Art Blue, an Athabascan Indian from Manitoba told us. He had been a fighter pilot in Korea before becoming a psychotherapist. He also told us about the Snake dance of the Hopis, in which he had taken part.

Long before we learned about Aby Warburg's *Lecture on Serpent Rtual*, we heard him describe the risk taken by the one dancing with a rattlesnake in his mouth for half an hour: "Either you die, or you become the snake". At the end of his lecture, Aby Warburg analysed the intelligence displayed in this ritual:

> The snake cult [shows] the change from real and substantial symbolism which appropriates the actual gestures to that symbolism which exists in thought alone.[5]

This "change" is at the heart of our work with madness and trauma.

There eventually comes a day, often after we make one of those blunders Winnicott talked about, when we suddenly embody the lawless agency which broke "the tool with the names". Then, the only thing to do is to get a firm grip on it and let your mouth turn the deathly message into a source of life. To illustrate, I often cite the following story.[6]

I was accused, by a patient hospitalised with schizophrenia, of being Mengele and of having carried out experiments on her; her mother had been assassinated at Auschwitz. I don't remember the details of the session where, when she threw this accusation at me, I answered that, as I was a young analyst, I had experimented "with her", but not "on her". To my great surprise, she came to the next session quite serene.

When she was four years old, she had seen her mother being arrested by the militia, and she was the only one who knew that her mother had been deported as a Jew, and not as a political militant. In the interval between the two sessions, I had a dream in which she appeared in the guise of Anne Frank. Defying all the rules, I told her about my dream at our next session. Soon afterwards, she left the hospital.

Could we say that the act of taking firm hold of the murderous agency was transformed into "symbolism which exists in thought", making it possible to inscribe, like Anne Frank's *Diary* does, a story to which there was no other witness? In such cases, Gaetano Benedetti speaks of "therapeutic dreams", and he advises us to tell them to the patient, since they are rooted in the session. He is not the only one to hold this opinion.

Art Blue told us about a version of the "vision quest" intended for youngsters, practised by Canadian Indians from the Northwest Territories. In certain circumstances—no doubt critical, the youth goes off alone into the bush for several days. Upon his return, he is met by an elder who had a dream about him and who recounts it. Only then is it possible for what the youth saw and heard to take shape, by being linked to the dream of the other. This ritual is called the "path of secrets". The Indians say that little by little the secrets of childhood are revealed to more and more people, and this is how myths are created.

In Lakota, the term for "medicine man" means "the one who fixes", who repairs the social link at points of rupture—of which they have had more than their share. They do not employ the word "shaman", so fashionable today, nor the hallucinogenic drugs of which "New Age" Californians are so fond. They insist that the only thing that counts is each person's desire to live, a desire they have no need to interpret.

"Don't believe a word he says", Joe's assistant, Stanley Red Bird, would tell us. Stanley, who had been a rodeo champion, was one of the cofounders, with Jerry Mohatt, of the Sinte Gleska College. And he would add: "He talks rubbish, he's really an other". That is to say, someone who can make contact with what Nanosy called "another world".

On the warpath

An association of practices between a North American Indian rite and the psychoanalysis of madness emerged in an interdisciplinary seminar organised in New York in 1929 by Harry Stack Sullivan,[7] a psychoanalyst of psychosis. In his introduction, Sullivan stated that he had made a discovery while working with young patients labelled "schizophrenic": "Their analyses of social interactions invisible in normal life involve all the different social sciences". Dolfi, Aby and children who made themselves heard in the patients I mentioned, who witnessed denied or falsified events, are proof of this.

Prior to arriving at Austen Riggs, we had never heard of Sullivan. He was first described to us as having had an original way of choosing attendants in his work with hospitalised patients, selecting sensitive individuals and encouraging them to tell stories about themselves.

There was precedent for such a practice, as Sullivan learned at the 1929 conference I mentioned, where he heard anthropologist Edward Sapir talk about the "Crazy Dogs Society" of the Plains Indians, where youngsters formed small groups of three or four individuals before setting out on the warpath. Then they vowed to fight to the death if one of them was killed, and sealed their pact of loyalty by confessing past "irregularities".

Since the anthropologist made a parallel between this practice and "the psychotic and traumatic crises we see in our own wars", Sullivan recounted his experience in the psychiatric hospital. The confession of "mistakes" made by attendants at crucial moments—blunders, as Winnicott called them—starts to weave a social link with violent or withdrawn patients. Wittgenstein himself had recourse to such a confession.

In 1937, he set out on the warpath against totalitarianism and anti-Semitism. He had come back from Russia disillusioned, only to witness the rise of Nazism in Austria. It was then that he made a secret "confession" to close friends, admitting his guilt about having denied his family's Jewish identity, disguised by his grandfather's conversion to Protestantism.

An association of practices was also helpful to British analyst William Rivers in treating soldiers sent back from the front during the Great War, as I mentioned to Emmanuelle and Nanosy at the end of our meeting.

Captain William Rivers, analyst of war traumas

A famous neurologist, anthropologist and lecturer at Cambridge University, Rivers discovered the two functions of the *therapon* while treating men who went mad in the trenches. In 1915 he returned from the Salomon Islands, where he recorded the funeral rites of Head Hunters, before such rites disappeared. Too old to be drafter in France, Rivers was recruited as a psychiatrist at Craiglockhart Hospital in Scotland, a military hospital for shellshocked officers returning from the front.

Among them was the poet Siegfried Sassoon,[8] who walked away from the front, threw all his medals into a river, and wrote a letter to the House of Commons to stop the war. The psychiatrist was handed the formal request of either declaring him psychotic, to the detriment of his psyche, or declaring him sane, in which case he risked court martial.

Faced with this dilemma, Rivers created an interval for frontline psychoanalysis, at the end of which Sassoon decided to go back to his men on the front line, after one of them, who had just been killed, appeared to him "out of the gloom" in his hospital room. He would come back alive, unlike the young poet Wilfred Owen,[9] another patient at Craiglockhart, killed on November 4, 1918.

How Rivers became an analyst of war traumas is recounted in a literary work, the novel *Regeneration Trilogy*[10] by Pat Barker. She wrote it based on Rivers's case notes and his ethnologist's field diary. In the Trilogy, we see Rivers inventing means of access to unspeakable scenes while reading Freud and simultaneously modifying his technique. Rivers also benefits from the teaching of the medicine man Njiru, his informant on the Solomon Islands and "an outstanding psychotherapist".

In 1918, Rivers's article in *The Lancet*[11] distinguishes between "repression" and "suppression", the two types of unconscious—repressed and cut out—identified by Freud. At Craiglockhart, Rivers is constantly challenged by his patients, especially by one very recalcitrant officer. This man who hardly speaks suddenly asks Rivers why he stutters when he is stressed. The analyst proposes that they change places—literally. The traumatised officer now plays the role of the analyst: "When did it start? Where?" Rivers reveals what he has already published: "When I was six... at the top of the stairs..." "—You were raped?" asks the patient who was abused by a pastor at about that age "—No". Rivers is the one who falls silent now, unable to remember. Their joint research begins.

A scene emerges, where the officer sees himself in a shell hole, picking up the blue eye of his buddy killed by an explosion. Another scene emerges for the analyst while he is visiting his younger sister Katharine. Their father was a pastor and speech therapist, focusing on correcting stammering. But he missed that of his own son. While Rivers and Katharine are talking, she mentions in passing a painting hanging at the top of the stairs in their childhood home. Through her eyes, her brother can see the scene suppressed by the dissociation of an experience cut away until then.

The painting shows the amputation on a ship, with no anaesthetic other than rum, of the leg of an ancestor whose name was also William Rivers. He was the sailor who killed the man who killed Admiral Nelson in 1805, at the Battle of Trafalgar. The traumatic memory comes back to Rivers. He is six years old, has had his hair cut by a barber for the first time that day, and cried loudly in the barber shop, exasperating his father. At home, his father lifted him up to show him the painting, saying: "He didn't cry. He didn't make a sound". The child who bore the same name cut himself off from this scene, just like his ancestor had absented himself in order to bear the amputation.

Rivers believes this to be the source of his determination to help men returning from the front to express what they hold back behind their clenched teeth. He indirectly inspired British analyst Wilfried Bion, through Bion's second psychoanalyst, John Rickman, another veteran of the First World War, and Rivers's disciple.

Bion meets the ghost of Captain Bion in Los Angeles

Bion nicknamed his first analyst FIP, Feel It in the Past, since he was always sending him into the past, instead of dealing with his ever-present war. A tank commander at 20, awarded the Victoria Cross and the *Légion d' Honneur*, Bion described his state of mind after the Armistice in these terms:

> I did not see that peacetime was no time for me. I did not know... that wartime was also no time for me. I was 24 years old; no good for war, no good for peace, and too old to change. It was truly terrifying. Sometimes it burst out in sleep. Terrified. What about? Nothing, nothing.

This passage is taken from a manuscript found unfinished[12] at the time of his death in 1979, when he was 82 years old. His wife, Francesca, admitted that he had nightmares every night. In 1968, when he was over 70, he chose exile to Los Angeles to escape "the cozy domesticity of England", and to record his experience of war in three autobiographical books: *All My Sins Remembered*,[13] *the Long Week-End, 1897–1917*,[14] and *A Memoir of the Future*[15] written as a work of fiction.

I believe Bion's desire to do this was partly prompted in Los Angeles by echoes of the American accent of the soldiers who had fought by his side.

Moreover, the fact that Kurt Vonnegut's bestseller *Slaughterhouse-Five*[16] was published in 1969 may have provided further incitement.

Vonnegut's hero, Billy Pilgrim, is a quixotic character. Back from captivity, like his author who was held prisoner in the cellar of a Dresden slaughterhouse while the city was bombarded and destroyed in February 1945, Pilgrim lives a normal life in a small American town. But, oddly, once in a while he walks through a "time window", is abducted by space aliens, and has "memories of the future". This expression, often repeated in the novel, probably inspired Bion's title *A Memoir of the Future*.

In this final book, in which a multitude of characters carry on a dialogue—Alice, Robin, Captain Bion, Myself, P.A. (the psychoanalyst) and different ages of his life, including his embryonic cells called "Somites"— Bion writes: "I died at Ypres, at Cambrai (on November 20, 1917), at Amiens (on August 6, 1918)", when the entire tank crew under his command was killed. At the end of the second part of *A Memoir*, called "The Past Presented", the psychoanalyst P.A. converses with his own ghost, Ghost of P.A., to whom he admits: "I was so afraid to meet you".

It takes time to consent to meet the cut-out parts of ourselves. Activated by surviving images, they operate in survival mode and seem laughable from an ordinary perspective. This explains why Bion only made this ghostly memories public at an advanced age.

The first part of *A Memoir*, called "The Dream", portrays a nightmare in which England is invaded by a totalitarian country embodied by an emotionless character: Man. After the analyst has dared to speak to his own ghost, the third part of the book, "The Dawn of Oblivion" opens onto the future.

Speaking of the diaries kept for patients and their families, Nanosy said: "...by writing you project yourself into the future: one day he will read it, one day his wife or his children will want to read [it]. And that gives us hope that maybe he'll get well". When images that survived the catastrophe can be addressed to someone, they stop haunting their host and recede into the past.

As Bion said, "You can't forget what you can't remember, and things spin out of control".[17] But if an other manifests his presence in this catastrophic zone, time can regain its symbolic function.

Reading Bion's later works helps us understand the originality of his analytic practice, regarded with scepticism by his colleagues, although their author headed the Tavistock Clinic and was president of the British Psychoanalytic Society.

His theoretical books, written before his exile, give brief examples of sessions with difficult patients. Attentive to facial expression, posture and tone of voice, he names his own impressions in the present of the interaction, since causality cannot function in the arrested time of trauma. What his first analyst would have said: "You're traumatised because in your childhood..." invariably solicits the same answer: "I know it, but it doesn't change anything".

Change occurs when interferences happen with analogous zones in the analyst. "Trauma speaks to trauma", Jean-Max Gaudillière liked to say. In his 1970s seminars with Brazilian analysts,[18] Bion asserted that "one 'is' not a psychoanalyst, but 'becomes' one, as required in each case, with his personality". His own personality was shaped by his exile from his native India at the age of ten, alone, to be schooled in England; and then by his voluntary enrolment in the war at eighteen. Another one of his famous phrases is: "Transference is transient".

Such moments of transference are referred to in the video testimonies above, "when being there is what counts". I have punctuated them with Thomas Salmon's four principles: proximity, immediacy, hope and simplicity.

They established the ground for the future psychoanalysis of madness and trauma, and were applied by Salmon himself on the Vosges Front in 1918, "to enable the speechless to speak".

This therapeutic process can be seen over and over in the above testimonies, but first, let's take a closer look at the phrase "to enable the speechless to speak", which involves the great difficulty, for both participants, of coming face to face with what "leaves one speechless". The shock can be so great that it induces a delusion, as happens after a war or when coming out of a coma. Enabling the speechless to speak often gives voice to a folly that leaves us speechless.

Except if this delusion is taken to be an inquiry into the unspeakable. To explore this possibility, I listened to researchers who have themselves experienced a period of madness. Aby Warburg wrote that the intelligence at work in his folly was no different than that which produced his scientific work. John Nash,[19] the hero of the film *A Beautiful Mind*, made a similar comment, saying that the same mind could rave about extraterrestrial beings and win the Nobel Prize for economics.

To help me shed more light on this complex subject, I shall refer, in turn, to the work of Auguste Comte, linking his "cerebral crisis" to political upheaval; to Erwin Schrodinger, who advises us to make use of the interferences occurring in the sessions; and to René Thom, who theorises "morphogenesis", the creation of shapes on the edge of catastrophes. I will also have the support of a young woman whose delusion was an investigation of events that leave one speechless.

Notes

1 Frazer, J. G., *The Golden Bough: A Study in Magic and Religion*, Oxford: Oxford Paperbacks, 2009.
2 Wittgenstein, L., Remarks on Frazer's Golden Bough, in *Wittgenstein, Sources and Perspectives*, Ithaca, NY: Cornell University Press, 1979.

3 Mohatt, G. and Eagle Elk, J., *The Price of a Gift. A Lakota Healer's Story*, Lincoln: Nebraska University Press, 2000.
4 Lacan, J., *The Seminar of Jacques Lacan. Book VII. The Ethics of Psychoanalysis 1959–1960*, London: Routledge, 1992.
5 Warburg, A., "A Lecture on Serpent Ritual", op. cit.
6 Davoine, F., *Wittgenstein's Folly*, New York: YBK Publishers, 2012.
7 Sullivan, H. S., "Schizophrenic Individuals As a Source of Data for Personality Research", in *Schizophrenia as a Human Process*, London: W.W. Norton, 1974.
8 Sassoon, S. (1886–1967). *The War Poems*, London: Faber & Faber, 2014.
9 Owen, W. (1893–1918). *The War Poems*, London: Sinclair-Stevenson, 1994.
10 Barker, P., *Regeneration Trilogy*, London: Penguin Books, 1992.
11 Rivers, Captain W., The Repression of War Experience, in *The Lancet*, February 2, 1918.
12 Bion, W., *All My Sins Remembered*, London: Karnac, 1985.
13 "Be all my sins remembered" is the last verse of Hamlet's soliloquy "To be or not to be", Act 3, Sc.1.
14 Bion, W., *The Long Week-End*, London: Karnac, 1982.
15 Bion, W., *A Memoir of the Future*, London: Karnac, 1981.
16 Vonnegut, K., *Slaughterhouse-Five*, Piscataway, NJ: Research & Education Association, 1996.
17 Bion, W. R., *Clinical Seminars and Other Works*, London: Karnac, 1987; Sao Paulo lectures, 1978.
18 Bion, W. R., *Brazilian Lectures*, London: Routledge, 1990.
19 *A Beautiful Mind*, film, Howard, R. (dir.), 2001, based on the novel by Sylvia Nasar, New York: Touchstone, 1998.

Chapter 9

Madness and Historical Upheavals

The Auguste Comte house

When I joined Alain Touraine's sociology laboratory at the end of 1968, it was located at number 10, rue Monsieur le Prince, in Auguste Comte's house. The following year it moved into the *Maison des Sciences de l'Homme*, where different centres of the École des Hautes Études en Sciences Sociales were relocated, on the former site of the Cherche-Midi prison, across from the Lutetia Hotel. Had I read Paul Arbousse-Bastide's book *Auguste Comte et la folie*[1] (Auguste Comte and Madness) I could have invoked the authority of the inventor of the word "sociology", to justify our subsequent decision to work in different public psychiatric hospitals, and my choice of Don Quixote as our ally in conducting our weekly seminar entitled "Madness and the Social Link".

"What are you getting yourselves into?" Touraine used to ask us. But the day came when he resumed what we were doing by saying simply: "Mad people are the subject of social sciences". At the time, we didn't know that Harry Stack Sullivan had made a similar statement at the 1929 International Psychoanalytic Congress.

In a letter written to Dr G. Audiffret in 1855, Auguste Comte speaks of madness as a dynamic process related to catastrophic ruptures of the social link. He describes it as an "excess of subjectivity triggered by political upheavals or epidemics, which disturb the unity of the self as well as the connection between the living and the dead, to a lesser or greater degree depending on the person".

In fact, he experienced such a disturbance himself. When, in 1826, at the age of 28, he was hospitalised in the Esquirol clinic to be treated for his "cerebral crisis",[2] he ran away, judging the "empirical medication" he was receiving disastrous. He overcame "the illness, and especially its remedies", thanks to the affectionate care he received at home, and to his personal reflections.

Around the time of his birth in 1798, and in the century that followed, political upheavals abounded. This explains his "sociological definition" of the brain, very surprising coming from a positivist: "It is an organ through

DOI: 10.4324/9781003257592-11

which the dead act upon the living". In *System of Positive Polity*, published in 1854, he claimed that his "cerebral crisis" was what drove his research, and he advised the reader to read *Don Quixote*:

> Cervantes' admirable composition describes deeply the way in which our emotions modify our sensations, sketching out the true theory of madness before any biologist.

Indeed, Don Quixote is the subject of the investigation of the "political upheavals" experienced by Cervantes for five years in the war against the Turks, and then during his five other years of enslavement in Algiers. As he explores his author's traumas thanks to his folly, the knight himself becomes an analyst twice: in the first novel for Cardenio, the madman of the Sierra Morena, and in the second novel, for doña Rodriguez, duenna of honour of the perverse duchess.

When he published his first novel[3] at the age of 58, Cervantes entrusted his "dry, shrivelled, whimsical offspring, full of thoughts of all sorts and such as never came into any other imagination"—as he describes him in the Author's Preface—with hallucinating his own ten years of misfortune before his return to Spain at the age of 30, only to be ignored and forgotten. At 64, he published the second *Don Quixote*, after finding out that other authors, jealous of his success, had paid a forger to write a terrible sequel to the knight's adventures, ridiculing his heroes. For this reason, Cervantes sends the knight off to take to the road again and to fight perversion.

Thus, Don Quixote becomes an analyst in the wild space of the mountain, and later at the ducal castle, where his frontline psychotherapy reveals the treason of Cardenio's and Doña Rodriguez' "high command", a factor identified by Jonathan Shay[4] as a major source of trauma. In the first novel, the young man is betrayed by his friend and suzerain, who has stolen his ladylove; in the second, the old woman reveals the Duke and Duchess' turpitude, covered over by the false generosity they show the knight.

These two episodes in which madness explores what Cervantes calls "our depraved era", brings to mind an example I have often cited.[5]

Your delusion is a search

A young woman I saw long ago at the psychiatric hospital still keeps in touch; I hear from her regularly. At the hospital, she was sometimes Satan and sometimes the Earth Goddess. Now, she enjoys her life and needs no medication. Recently, she summed up the long years of analysis she had with me by saying: "What I found most useful was not your theories, but the fragments of stories from books or from your own life that you told me". She also recalled that during our first meeting I had said: "Your delusion is a quest", and she added: "I remember that very well".

I remember very well entering the large common room at the hospital, where she was conversing with a "difficult" patient. I thought she was a trainee. When I asked: "Are you a psychologist?" she answered: "No. I am psychotic. And you, what are you doing here?" For the first time, to my usual answer: "I work here as a psychoanalyst", I added that I also worked at the EHESS, the School for Advanced Studies in the Social Sciences, where I was giving a seminar called "Madness and the Social Link". She promptly replied: "Speaking of madness and the social link, I have to tell you that when he was at war, serving in the Italian army, my father was the sole survivor of a massacre during the Battle of El Alamein in 1942". I immediately remembered that my own father had also escaped the massacre of French hostages at a place called Terre Noire, on the Italian side of Little Saint-Bernard Pass on August 17, 1944, on the right side of the road leading to the land of her ancestors.

I didn't say anything, but I took note of the coincidence. She added: "When I leave the hospital I will see you at the clinic". When I stopped working at the hospital after the retirement of the head doctor who had hired us and then accompanied us for 30 years, she came to see me at my private office until she was ready to resume her life. She stayed in touch and called me during the pandemic to advise me to read the *Decameron*.

Her folly had been an escape from severe abuses, and her delusion was indeed research on the "banality of evil", to use a term coined by Hanna Arendt. But one day the thread was suddenly broken during a session in which our mutual ghosts entered the stage. She arrived very determined, saying: "My mission on earth is coming to an end, the aliens have ordered me to join them in a month". I immediately thought of the young people murdered at El Alamein and at Terre Noire, but it was useless to speak of the past now, since, in the present, her suicide was imminent. Given this urgency, I replied: "The aliens live so far away that their message takes many years to reach us. Ah!" she exclaimed, "Einstein!"

The tension left her body, she smiled. Time had set itself in motion again. Thank you, Einstein!

Interferences at the edges of catastrophes

To bolster this joint research when "the time is out of joint",[6] we also relied on researchers in the field of exact sciences, like Erwin Schrödinger, Austrian physicist and poet who discovered the canonical equations of quantum physics, and won the 1933 Novel Prize in physics. In his Tarner Lectures,[7] given in Cambridge in 1956, he extended an appeal to psychotherapists. Given the fact that light particles are disturbed by observation when encountering other light particles, and that only their interaction can be studied, he advised "the relatively new science of psychology" to focus on similar interferences instead of adopting a neutral, "objective" position. He too was speaking from experience.[8]

After the Anschluss, he was the only non-Jew who resigned his position. Since he was harassed by the new Nazi regime, he and his wife Anny left the country secretly, ending up in Dublin in 1939. There, Anny showed signs of psychic disorder and was treated by psychiatrist Maurice O'Drury, Wittgenstein's disciple.

Our sons, who were science students, laughed at us when we mentioned Schrödinger. Still, we then turned quite shamelessly to the catastrophe theory of mathematician René Thom, who also liked to address non specialists. In his interview with Emile Nöel, published under the title "To Predict Is Not to Explain",[9] he reveals that he conceived his theory after a crisis following his winning of the Fields Medal in 1958. His competitor was John Nash, whose madness emerged a short time later.[10] Familiar with extraterrestrial beings—like the young woman I mentioned above, and like the inventor of the incompleteness Theorem, Kurt Gödel[11] at the end of his life—Nash was awarded the 1994 Nobel Prize for economics.

Since madness tries to inscribe what cannot be said, it is not surprising to see it appear among scientists who invent new paradigms and create scientific revolutions. René Thom defines catastrophes as "breaks in continuity" which give rise, on their edges, to forms that can be expressed in mathematical language.

And why not in everyday language? "When the tool with the names is broken", Wittgenstein says, one cannot help showing what cannot be said by surviving forms emerging at the edges of fracture: voices, visions, nightmares and reviviscences, subjecting the analyst as well to intrusive impressions. This is the interference on which Schrodinger advises us to focus. And then we should point it out to our co-researcher, making speech possible on the edge of silence.

The wall of silence

Dori Laub[12] used to say that in these circumstances the first question we are asked is: "Who are you" so that I should venture to talk to you? The quest for knowledge in this transference seeks indications of our ability to overcome the break with the ordinary world. These clues often remain unnoticed by the analyst, but are identified by those who are experienced in deciphering the "Sound of silence", referred to in Simon and Garfunkel's famous song.[13] Replying: "And you, who do you think I am?" is useless, because the subject who thinks in this manner is yet to be constituted. For it to emerge, the validity of the observation must be confirmed thanks to a minimal interference. When this "nod of the head occurs", the ensuing exploration will often involve zones of silence going back several generations.

If you had told me in the 1970s that my grandfather, a stretcher-bearer in the Great War, or my parents, who were in the Resistance in Savoie during the next World War, were traumatised, I would have stared at you blankly, not knowing what you were talking about. It's true that my grandfather never talked about the men he was transporting on his stretcher; my father had nightmares until his death, at 103, which always surprised him; and my mother would suddenly stop talking, without an explanation. But all this was normal.

Normal and ordinary, like my first months as an embryo, after her arrest when she was crossing the demarcation line in secret, and her incarceration in the Chalon-sur-Saône and Autun prisons before her departure for Compiègne early in 1943. The fact that she barely escaped deportation trains was normal too. I only ever heard her say two things on that subject. The first was about the chocolate bars distributed to the female inmates of the crowded cell by the bishop of Autun: "Although I really wanted to save it, I couldn't help eating it at once". The second concerned her companions: "If I had been Jewish, I wouldn't be here now", And neither would I.

Afterwards, what I was told over and over was: "It was the war, you were born during the war", and that explained everything. The next few years, between 1943 and 1945 were marked by fleeing, hiding, bullets, bombs dropped from above Little Saint-Bernard Pass, as well as joyous times that I recounted to my Lacanian analyst as they were told to me, in random sequence. He managed to produce a few puns and some signifiers, without asking any questions. Perhaps the word "trauma" was not part of his theory, except to change it into "trouma", and so what?

Was it acting out on our part when we set out across war fields and paths that cut through cemeteries left by immemorial battles, to reach the Prémontré Hospital in a region repeatedly devastated since before the Franco-Pussian war of 1870? The poet Siegfried Sassoon told his analyst William Rivers[14] that in the trenches he saw "the skulls of ancient and future wars: those of Marlborough's armies and the ploughed up skulls of this war".

Not everyone has access to such a memory of the future. In our School of psychoanalysis, we happened to give a presentation of our interactions with the "residents" of Prémontré who often spoke about the war in the present tense. Someone interrupted, and a deep voice asked those present: "Who are these young analysts who go to the psychiatric hospital to be psychoanalysed?" In other words: "Go back on the couch".

But we chose instead to cross the ocean in search of other allies. I have already recounted our meeting with Sioux medicine men on the Rosebud Reserve in South Dakota, thanks to Jerry Mohatt. We had met him at Austen Riggs Center, dedicated to the psychoanalysis of psychoses. In 1979, we had been invited there by John Muller, Jim Gorney and philosopher William Richardson, to speak about Lacan. This is how we discovered a tradition of analysis of trauma and psychosis we knew nothing about: "frontline psychotherapy".

And this is where we heard for the first time, the names of Harry Stack Sullivan and Frieda Fromm-Reichmann. They were introduced to us as analysts who worked with patients considered unsuitable for psychoanalysis. Later on we heard of Thomas Salmon, who invented his principles in a time of war, immigration and an epidemic.

Notes

1 Arbousse-Bastide, P., Auguste Comte et la folie, in *Les sciences de la folie*, R. Bastide (Ed.), Paris: Mouton, 1972.
2 Gouhier, H., *La Vie d'Aguste Comte*, Paris: Vrin, 1997; Pickering, M., *Auguste Comte: An Intellectual Biography*, Cambridge: Cambridge University Press, 1993.
3 Cervantes, M., *Don Quixote I* (1605), *Don Quixote II* (1615), op. cit. See also: Davoine, A. F., *Figting Melancholia*, London: Kanrac, 2016; *A Word to the Wise*, London: Routledge 2018, op. cit.
4 Shay, J., *Achilles in Vietnam*, New York: Scribner, 1995.
5 Davoine, F. and Gaudillière, J.-M., *History beyond Trauma*, op. cit.
6 Shakespeare, W., *Hamlet*, New York: Simon & Shuster, 2003. Act I, sc. 5, v. 189.
7 Schrödinger, E., *What Is life? With Mind and Matter and Autobiographical Sketches*, Cambridge: Cambridge University Press, 2012.
8 Moore, W., Schrödinger, *Life and Thought*, Cambridge: Cambridge University Press, 1989.
9 Thom, R., To *Predict Is Not to Explain*, Toronto: Thombooks Press, 2016.
10 Nasar, S., *A Beautiful Mind*, op. cit.
11 Wang, H., *Reflections on Kurt Gödel*, Cambridge, MA, and London: The MIT Press, 1987.
12 Laub, D., *Une clinique de l'extrême*, Le Coq-Héron, Érès, no. 220.
13 Simon and Garfunkel, "The Sound of Silence", song, 1966.
14 Barker, P., *Regeneration Trilogy*, op. cit.

Chapter 10

Frontline Psychoanalysts

Harry Stack Sullivan: "we are all simply much more human than otherwise"

In Chicago, where Sullivan studied medicine before the First World War, 9 million immigrants had arrived since the beginning of the century. It was there that he met the researchers of the Chicago School of Sociology, and Jane Addams[1] who founded Hull House in 1899, a beautiful house in the middle of a slum, offering refuge to immigrant women and their babies, and a place to school their children. When she died in 1935, a huge crowd followed her coffin in the streets.

During the war, Sullivan was liaison officer at the Saint Elizabeth Hospital, whose director, William Alanson White, encouraged interaction between the clinical approach and social sciences. In the 1920s, Sullivan became an analyst for young schizophrenics at the Sheppard Pratt Hospital in Baltimore, and later continued in private practice.

His books,[2] including *Schizophrenia as a human Process* and *The Fusion of Psychiatry and Social Sciences*, were transcribed from recordings by Ellen Swick Perry,[3] his assistant and future biographer. When we met her, she told us that a short time before his death in Paris in 1948, Sullivan had told her: "Had I benefitted from the electric and chemical treatments in vogue today, I would be a vegetable in a psychiatric hospital".

In 1909, at the age of 17, while attending Cornell University, he was hospitalised at the Bellevue Hospital in New York after being arrested by the police with a gang of delinquents. There, he had the good fortune of undergoing therapy with Abraham Brill, one of the first analysts in the United States, who not only helped him on that occasion, but planted the seeds of his future vocation.

The parallels in their stories are evident. Brill had emigrated from Galicia at 15, arriving in New York penniless. At 17, Sullivan did not have a dime either. He had been brought up on a farm by his grandmother, who had fled the potato famine in Ireland and had lost a baby and her first husband on the boat bringing them to America. Sullivan himself was an only child,

DOI: 10.4324/9781003257592-12

whose siblings had died in infancy due to unsanitary conditions in his family's neighbourhood.

That year, in 1909, Brill was accompanying Freud, Jung and Ferenczi on their visit to Clark University. Brill always minimised his success with young borderline or schizophrenic patients, fearing criticism for his deviant practices. He later became President of the American Psychoanalytic Association. On the contrary, Sullivan and Frieda Fromm-Reichmann always defended their use of the unorthodox practice known as "intensive psychodynamic analytic psychotherapy for psychosis". This new approach to madness had been prompted by the publication in 1907 of the autobiography of a former patient, Clifford Beers,[4] under the title *A Mind that Found Itself*.

Beers was hospitalised in appalling conditions after his studies at Yale. When he recovered from his delusions thanks to another patient, he was encouraged by William James to publish an account of his experience. The immediate success of his book contributed to the creation, in 1909, by Beers and Adolf Myers, of the National Committee for Mental Hygiene, to change the treatment of madness. Committee members would later include William Alanson White, Harry Stack Sullivan and Thomas Salmon, who was its medical director at the outbreak of the Great War. The reform of psychiatric hospitals started by Salmon, and his innovative practices with traumatised soldiers, were influenced by this new direction that preceded Freud's arrival.

When he landed in New York in 1909, Freud told Jung and Ferenczi: "They don't realize that we are bringing them the plague". He did not know, no doubt, that an infectious agent already circulated in the psychotherapy of trauma, that he had abandoned in 1897.

Among the analysts who immigrated to the United States in the 1930s—fleeing Naziism—Frieda Fromm-Reichmann[5] stood out: she was familiar with the frontline psychotherapy advocated by Thomas Salmon and Harry Stack Sullivan. At the start of the Great War, at 26, she was working as a young neurologist in a hospital ward filled with soldiers with head injuries—a situation not unlike that of the young Intensive Care doctors who spoke to me at the height of the pandemic. As Lucie said: "I had just been made Chief anaesthesiologist, I had had my position for four months and I was thinking:—a pandemic to start my career, I'm not equipped for that, I won't be able to do it".

Frieda Fromm-Reichmann: "everything is transference"

Young Frieda Fromm-Reichmann might have felt the same way in her home town of Keonigsberg, at the hospital where brain-injured soldiers kept arriving. She had trained under neuropsychiatrist Kurt Goldstein, and was interested by his research on schizophrenia and war traumas. Soon she was heading the ward—unofficially, since she was a woman. With the support of her patients, she escaped the attention of Prussian inspectors. After the war, she joined Kurt Goldstein at his Frankfurt clinic for two years, undertook analytic training at the Berlin Psychoanalytic Institute, and opened a clinic in Heidelberg in 1928.

Her unique experience made her wary of traditional psychoanalysts whom she often considered "dandified". She was more familiar with Georg Groddeck's approach[6]—an approach based on the relationship between body and psyche. She would visit his sanatorium in nearby Baden-Baden, where she met Ferenczi, who had been drafted to work as a military doctor in a Budapest hospital. Like Frieda, he was interested in the traumatic origins of psychosis and war neuroses. When Hitler came to power in 1933, Frieda took leave of her patients and crossed the Rhine with a suitcase for a weekend leave from which she had no intention of returning.

Two years later she immigrated to the United States, where she found a summer job in a rehabilitation clinic for diplomats near Washington. The director, Dr Dexter Bullard, realised the value of what she could contribute and asked her to create a centre for the psychoanalysis of schizophrenia. He built a cottage on the hospital grounds for her, where she made her home until her death in 1957. It was there, at Chestnut Lodge,[7] that many analysts of psychosis and trauma received their training; among them, Otto Will, Martin Cooperman, Harold Searles and Gaetano Benedetti.

Frieda's patient Joanne Greenberg wrote a fictionalised account of her analysis with "doctor Fried"—an alias for Fromm-Reichmann—from the time she entered Chestnut Lodge in a delusional state at 16, until she started university. Her book, whose title, *I Never Promised You a Rose Garden*,[8] was a phrase her analyst would say, became a bestseller a few years after its publication in 1964. It reveals the changes Frieda made to traditional treatment, while taking Freud's doctrine into account.

When I would meet her at conferences, Joanne Greenberg (Frieda's former patient) used to describe her analyst's animated face, her bursts of laughter, the stories she told, and her favourite sentence: "When there is no transference, everything is transference". Intensive Care doctors and nurses know this when they speak to apparently unconscious patients, because "They hear what is said to them". Frieda's statement opens a way out of the impasse in which the analysis of psychosis has remained trapped.

This was the orientation which awaited us at the Austen Riggs Center, located in Stockbridge, Massachusetts, where we arrived on a freezing cold winter day in late December 1979.

Martin Cooperman: the analysis of madness takes a week

The Director, Otto Will, had just retired; Martin Cooperman was the Medical Director of the Centre. Our presentation was deemed typically French.

We had been invited to speak about the death instinct in Lacan's teaching, and we spoke of his seminar *The Ethics of Psychoanalysis*,[9] citing his remarks on Sophocles' play *Antigone*, which contains the concept "a space between two deaths". Based on our experience in psychiatric hospitals, we were contending that the psychoanalysis of psychosis takes place in that very space: between death without a tomb and the symbolic inscription of a name on a grave. We were asked a single question: "Your presentation was fantastic, but how do you go about it?"

Instead of grumbling about Anglo-Saxon pragmatism, we were relieved to finally be able to tell stories about our practice which, in the theoretical perspective of our Sociology Centre and in our psychoanalytic School, were considered to have merely anecdotal value. We were also delighted to spend the afternoon hearing stories about their successes and failures with various theoretical approaches.

When Martin Cooperman[10] invited us into his office, he went to a drawer and took out his photograph in military uniform, as a Navy flight surgeon during the Second World War. He wanted to show us that he had visited Paris before leaving for the Pacific front, where his aircraft carrier, the Wasp, was sunk at Guadalcanal. We were amazed by this spontaneous personal revelation inconceivable among our colleagues, when he surprised us even more by declaring out of the blue:

> An analysis of madness takes a week, but it takes years to get to it. At first, the analyst hides behind his theories and the patient behind his symptoms, until they both come out of hiding and can finally meet.

Much of what he said was not clear to me, but I noticed his insistence on the here and now of the session.

What's more, interferences occurring in transference did not seem to shock him. The following summer, he was dozing during my presentation, in which I was using an example from my experience at Prémontré. Opening one eye, he interjected: "Foliadiou". I asked for a translation. "Good God!" he exclaimed, now fully awake. "You don't even understand your own language!" It took me some time to realise that he saw the moments of "folie à deux" as pivotal to the week it takes for healing psychosis, as he had said.

Otto Will: do you believe in psychoanalysis?

Our discussion with Otto Will was just as disconcerting. He asked us point blank: "Do you believe in psychoanalysis?" Then, without waiting for an answer, he told us the following story. When he came back from Guadalcanal, where he had fought in the war just like Cooperman, he undertook, "God knows why", an analysis with Sullivan, to whom he kept saying that he didn't believe in what they were doing. Until something happened.

He was then a physician in a military hospital, and had to take time off for stomach surgery. When he came back, feeling a bit weak, he sat down next to the bed of a soldier who was letting himself die, lying in a comatose stupor. Sitting beside him, Otto started to think out loud. As Emmanuelle said: "We speak to them because [they] hear even in a coma. We speak to them a lot. Each of us says whatever he wants". Otto Will noticed the sound of crackling sheets, and kept addressing himself to them week after week, thinking: "I'm losing my wits". Until the day the soldier came out of the coma. Otto then told Sullivan: "It's working, that thing that you do!"

Coincidentally, I had a similar experience at Prémonté five years earlier, where I had been in the habit of leaning for long periods against the radiator in the common room, next to a woman patient who never moved away from there. Like Otto Will, I said out loud anything that came to my mind. When I became pregnant for the first time in 1975, and stayed home because car travel was not recommended, I asked Jean-Max to take my place. One day the patient came out of a silence that had lasted years, and told him: "I heard a great YES, and now I can talk to you". This is her story, which I have often told[11]:

> Her mother was a lock keeper operating the locks on a canal in Northern France. Her father was away at war. Because her mother used to disappear often, the little girl followed her one day and saw her in the ditch of the neighbouring town with a German soldier. When she came back, the mother told the child: "You want to know what I do? Look!" and she lifted up her skirt. A short time later, the little girl threw herself into the canal. By chance, a sailor in the barge moored nearby, called "Just Think of It"—truth is stranger than fiction —, dove in the water to save her.

Where did the great YES she heard come from?

Premature knowledge

While writing these lines to connect Otto's story with mine for the first time, I wonder what made him stubbornly return to the bedside of a man who no longer looked human, and what made me keep standing next to a woman completely cut off from the world. Knowing that I was carrying our first son, is it possible that my mother's silence about the time we both spent in prison, before my birth, had been reawakened by this proximity? *Foliadiou!*

In such cases, Bion speaks of "premature knowledge" shown by embryos and infants. He describes it in *A Memoir of the Future*,[12] where his embryonic cells, called Somites, speak. Bion had probably read Laurence Sterne's 18th-century novel *Tristram Shandy*,[13] inspired by *Don Quixote*. The first two words of Sterne's book: "I wish", are spoken by the embryo of the future

Tristram, on the day of his half-failed conception, owing to the war between his parents. "I wish", followed by the subjunctive, does not express a present desire, but says: I would have liked them to "[mind] what they were about when they begot me".

The analyst who saves Tristram from the fate of a handicapped child is his uncle, Captain Toby, wounded at war, whose psychotherapy with Corporal Trim, his *therapon*, is analysed in the next volume of Sterne's novel. Having gone through a similar experience, Toby considers it his duty to tell his nephew the truth about his disastrous conception, recounted to him by his older brother Walter, Tristram's father. Throughout the novel, uncle Toby is the only person who takes a real interest in the boy, neglected by both his indifferent mother and his father who is fond of theories. Captain Toby is closely related to Captain Rivers and Captain Bion.

The infant's premature knowledge also played a role in Otto Will's life.

When we visited him near San Francisco, where he had retired, he told us this story. After his surgery, he continued to vomit and one day, during a session with Sullivan, he had to rush to the bathroom. His analyst helped him and suggested that he spend the night there, calling his wife to ask her to join him. After this unorthodox session, Otto had the idea of asking his mother a question about his first year of life, when his father had tuberculosis and was often confined to bed. He recovered after the family moved to New Mexico, where the climate was more favourable.

When he asked his elderly mother: "It could not have been easy to have a very sick husband and an infant to look after?" he was astounded to hear her answer: "But you were not with us, you were staying with relatives in the South". He was dumbfounded. Suddenly, a scene from the marriage of a cousin in the South became clear to him. "A black woman threw her arms around me laughing and crying, repeating: 'My baby, my baby!'" I was already six feet tall.

I thought: "These people in the South are very emotional" and I didn't ask any questions.

This is how facts, cut out by the unrepressed unconscious, made up of surviving images recorded early and shown, since they cannot be told, are transmitted, unless a therapist is able—like Sullivan did with Otto Will and Otto did with the soldier—to reach the dissociated scene through the present interaction.

Children of war

On the contrary, when veterans coming back from wars are greeted with questions like "Have you killed people? Have you committed atrocities?" they keep silent. But they cannot stop "the sound of silence" from entering the lives of their descendants, as this story I already told elsewhere[14] illustrates.

A young girl dressed in black came to see me after being discharged from the Sainte Anne psychiatric hospital in Paris, not knowing what she was looking for. She piled insults on herself to a degree I had never heard before, and told me in passing that her father had fought in the Algerian War. As a child, she had gone with him to banquets where he met with his war buddies.

I had just read *Achilles in Vietnam*[15] by Jonathan Shay—to which I will come back—and quoted a sentence from that book for her, in an assertive tone that surprised me: "These insults you're heaping on yourself are the ones thrown at your father, like buckets of dirty water, when he returned from Algeria. We, as psychoanalysts, bear responsibility, we have blood on our hands".

Disconcerted for a moment by this "we", for at the time I had not yet read a line of Freud, I regained my composure when I saw a faint smile forming on her lips. But she stood up to leave and I thought she would not return. When she came back on time for her next appointment, she wore a red broach on her black dress.

We conducted our joint research for a full year, after which she suddenly stopped coming. I thought she was hospitalised again, and I blamed my incompetence, as usual. A year later she rang my bell, without an appointment. She wanted to give me a beautiful book about a garden, and tell me that she was engaged. She had found a new path, "unexpectedly", as the Intensive Care workers told me.

In *Achilles in Vietnam*, Shay defines trauma as betrayal by your own side, that of your own high command, illustrated by Agamemnon who deprives Achilles of his share of the booty; but also betrayal by the home front, a trauma which is then passed on by parents to their children.

On men and war

A scene from a recent film by Laurent Bécue-Renard, *On Men and War*,[16] shows a little girl in a car anxiously scrutinising her father's closed face as he drives. The man is one of the war veterans filmed over a period of five years, with their wives and their children, in the San Francisco area which houses a Vet Centre. The director films group psychotherapy sessions conducted by a therapist who is himself a veteran, and shows what the Centre has to offer veterans' families. The film is dedicated to the director's grandfathers, whose photographs appear in the closing credits, showing them in the uniform of First World War officers.

One of the founders of these Vet Centres in the 1980s,[17] Art Blank, came to speak to us after a presentation of our book *History Beyond Trauma*[18] in New York. Working as an analyst today, Blank was a psychiatrist during the Vietnam War, from which he returned seriously traumatised. After consulting quite a few analysts, one more ignorant than the other about war, he finally found someone who understood.

This sparked the idea of creating centres for veterans, outside the network of specialised hospitals, to offer them psychotherapy, psychoanalytic or not, individual or in a group, family therapy, and other related services.

The personnel recruited for the centres must have first-hand experience of war, or have a family member who does. Today, several hundred Vet Centres exist all over the US for veterans of recent wars, including those on the front lines of the fight against Covid.

This concern with the particular care required by veterans with war traumas was already recognised, after the First World War, by Thomas Salmon, whose Principles I used to frame the six testimonies of frontline caregivers during the pandemic. Salmon formulated them during the summer of 1917.[19] He himself put them into practice when he was drafted at the end of the year and sent to the front lines in France. They serve in situations where we have to confront "another world"—as Nanosy says—in which our usual bearings have disappeared.

Thomas Salmon: letting the voiceless speak

"Fortune", so dear to Boccaccio, acquainted me with Thomas Salmon's name for the first time in 1995, when I spoke at a conference at the Washington School of Psychiatry, founded by Sullivan and Frieda Fromm-Reichmann. After my presentation, I remember asking point blank how it was that the older analysts at Austen Riggs spoke to us about their war experiences when they were teaching us about their practice with psychosis. No one answered.

Just as we were all leaving, a lady came up to us and introduced herself as Nancy Bakalar, psychiatrist in the U.S. Navy. She said: "Of course, you're familiar with the Salmon principles. He introduced them in France during the Great War". I mumbled that no, I did not know them at all. She promised to send us documents. Back in Paris, we received a package of documents, concerning frontline psychotherapy during the First and the Second World War.

I learned that Thomas Salmon had been sent somewhere along the front, with no military status, by the American Army, which was to enter the war at the end of 1917; his assignment was to bring back recommendations in anticipation of foreseeable psychic casualties. These documents formed the basis of a seminar we gave in 1996–1997, which led to our book *History beyond Trauma*, organised around Salmon's famous principles, which I believed to be the result of his trips back and forth between the United States and Europe in the summer of 1917.

Twenty years later, in 2017, I participated in the Washington Conference entitled "Psychoanalysis and Trauma", organised by Art Blank. This was when Art's colleague, Harold Kudler, respected expert in war traumas, suggested that I read Salmon's biography,[20] published in 1950. In this out-of-print book with a torn cover, I discovered a different story.

Born in 1870, Thomas Salmon was the descendent of French aristocrats exiled in England during the French Revolution. His parents immigrated to the United States, where life was not easy for them. Following in his father's footsteps, Thomas became a physician and treated the poor in rural areas without a fee. After his brother's and his parents' death, he returned to university, specialised in bacteriology and, in 1899, married Helen Ashley who was his lifelong partner.

Salmon's first assignment as a bacteriologist was to investigate a diphtheria epidemic in a psychiatric hospital. Although he was not a psychiatrist, this initial contact with madness determined the course of his life. Needing to provide for his family, he qualified for the public service and was appointed to Ellis Island between 1904 and 1906. His mission was to identify mental illness in immigrants, who would then be refused entry into the country. Salmon had a separate pavilion built for them, where they could feel safe before being diagnosed.

In 1912, he was named Medical Director of the National Committee for Mental Hygiene, and undertook to reform psychiatric hospitals. In fact, he was neither a military man nor a psychiatrist in 1917, when the American Army sent him on a two-month mission to England, where he probably met William Rivers in Scotland and became acquainted with his psychoanalysis of war traumas.

Although Salmon only treated patients after the war, he was aware of this approach thanks to his work on the Committee for Mental Hygiene, which promoted interdisciplinary exchanges. Therefore, it matters little whether his four principles were initially formulated as they would be later, since they constitute a solid pillar for the psychotherapy of traumas regardless of the place or the era, as we shall see.

Before reading his biography, I had forgotten that he had been sent to the Vosges front in December 1917, as a Major in the American Expeditionary Force. There, he trained young military doctors to work with soldiers close to the front lines, in an area connected with Base Hospital 117, set up in a castle near Neufchâteau.

Yet I had read *A War of Nerves. Soldiers and Psychiatrists in the Twentieth Century*,[21] by historian Ben Shephard, whose title echoes that of Bion's article "A War of Nerves", published in 1940. The book contained photos of William Rivers and Thomas Salmon, showing the latter in uniform in 1918, seated in his office on Base 117. But I had "closed my eyes" to his presence in France, displaying the "blindness of the seeing" Freud talked about, which had erased this fact from my consciousness. I also learned recently that he was a friend of Austen Riggs, the founder of the clinic named after him, where we discovered the continuity between his principles and the singularity of transference in the psychoanalysis of psychosis.[22]

Salmon's principles have been subject to various interpretations;

I will now describe how I make use of them when, as veteran Ludwig Wittgenstein says, "the tool with the names is broken".

Notes

1 Elshtain, J. B., *The Jane Addams Reader*, New York: Basic Books, 2012.
2 Sullivan, H. S., *Schizophrenia as a Human Process*, London: W.W. Norton, 1981; The *Fusion of Psychiatry and Social Sciences*, London: W.W. Norton, 1971.
3 Perry, E. S., *Psychiatrist of America: The Life of Henry Stack Sullivan*, Cambridge, MA: Belknap Press, 1982.
4 Beers, C., *A Mind that Found Itself*, Pittsburgh, PA: Pittsburgh University Press, 1981.
5 Fromm-Reichmann, F., *Principles of Intensive Psychotherapy*, Chicago, IL: University of Chicago Press, 1960.
6 Groddeck, G., *The Book of the It*, Eastford, CT: Martino Fine Books, 2015.
7 Hornstein, G., *To Redeem One Person is to Redeem the World. The Life of Frieda Fromm-Reichmann*, New York: The Free Press, 2000.
8 Greenberg, J., *I Never Promised You a Rose Garden*, New York: Signet, 1989.
9 Lacan, J., *The Seminar of Jacques Lacan*, (Book VII), London: W.W. Norton, 1997.
10 Cooperman, M., "Defeating Processes in Psychotherapy", 1969.
11 Davoine, F. and Gaudillière, J.-M., *History beyond Trauma*, op. cit.
12 Bion, W., *A Memoir of the Future*, op. cit.
13 Sterne, L., *Tristram Shandy*, op. cit.
14 Davoine, F., *Fighting Melancholia*, op. cit.
15 Shay, J., *Achilles in Vietnam*, New York: Touchstone, 1995.
16 Bécue-Renard, L., *On Men and War*, film, 2014.
17 Blank, A., Sonnenberg, S., and Talbott, J., *Stress Recovery in Vietnam Veterans*, Washington, DC: American Psychiatry Press, 1985.
18 Davoine, F. and Gaudillière, J-M., *History beyond Trauma*, op. cit.
19 Delaporte, S., Thomas W. Salmon. *Le Médecin des "sans voix" et des soldats, pour une autre psychiatrie (1872–1927)*, forthcoming. My thanks to the author for access to her in-depth study.
20 Bond, E., *Thomas Salmon, Psychiatrist*, New York: Norton, 1950.
21 Shephard, B., *A War of Nerves. Soldiers and Psychiatrists in the Twentieth Century*, Cambridge, MA: Harvard University Press, 2003.
22 I want to express my gratitude to Dominique Bo-Rohrer for this information.

Chapter 11

Salmon's Principles

These four principles delimit a specific space that makes it possible to reset in motion time knocked out of joint.

Proximity is first and foremost geographical. Near the front lines, the therapist and the patient "hear the sound of the canon" and share the same fear. "You want to know what war is?" my father would ask, "It's fear"—the first thing anaesthesiologists Jessica and Lucie said, as well as nurses Emmanuelle and Nanosy. In the analyst's office, proximity delimits a space of interferences at critical moments when trauma breaks through in the present time, allowing the emergence of a trustworthy but not infallible alterity, in the place of a ruthless agency which destroys all otherness.

Immediacy takes into account arrested time in someone's story, at the point of rupture specific to each of us. Since recourse to causality is useless when all symbolic bearings have collapsed, it is urgent to analyse what happens here and now, in the present interaction. From this perspective, Cooperman's comments become clear: "Your delusion is speaking to me and no one else, since there are only the two of us in the room". The same immediate presence is revealed in the testimonies. Jessica was fully present, she considered this a crucial moment for her. And Anne Lise asserted: "When there is urgent need, you do what has to be done first and you think later".

Expectancy, as in "life expectancy", not "expectation", as is often mistakenly believed, invalidates hopeless prognoses. To remain silent when asked: "Do you believe I will recover?" repeats the initial annihilation. This hopeful dimension is heard in all the testimonies: "You always think that a miracle can happen, something can change tomorrow, you keep going step by step, without giving up on the patient", Emmannuelle said. And Nanosy added: "By writing in the diaries you project into the future: one day he will read it, maybe he'll get well".

Simplicity needs no explanation. No jargon. Simplicity was Salmon's style.

DOI: 10.4324/9781003257592-13

An ignored practice

How is it possible that I didn't know these principles and that I was unaware of Salmon's wartime service in France? Was this ignorance due to rivalry between institutes? American psychoanalysis was harshly criticised in the Freudian School. Still, even in North America the analysts I mentioned were not highly regarded. They were forced to give their practice a complicated name: "intensive, psycho-dynamic analytic psychotherapy", since they were not granted use of the sacrosanct label "psychoanalysis". Moreover, "therapy" was deemed of lesser interest than "pure analytic discourse", at least in my training, which would explain the blacklisting of the authors I quoted.

We discussed this with psychoanalyst Claude Barrois, who was Chief of Psychiatry at the Val de Grâce military Hospital in Paris when we invited him to present his books, *Les névroses traumatiques* and *La psychanalyse du guerrier*[1] in our seminar. He was familiar with these principles, but could not tell us as the reasons for ignoring Thomas Salmon. The mystery was cleared up in 2013, when we participated in the seminar of First World War historian Stéphane Audoin-Rouzeau.[2] The other speaker was Stéphane Tison, historian of First World War psychiatry. After my presentation on the forward psychiatry introduced by Thomas Salmon, I asked him if anything equivalent existed in France during that period; he answered: "Nothing at all".

At the end of h that year, Stéphane Tison and Hervé Guillemain published their book *Du front à l'asile, 1914–1918*,[3] "From the front to the asylum", which describes the situation in France where the approach to war trauma remained mainly biological, with no psychoanalysts available to treat soldiers. The panacea of electric shock, known as faradisation and promoted by Clovis Vincent, was the treatment of choice. It also had proponents abroad, among whom Lewis Yealland in England, whose therapy is depicted by Pat Barker,[4] in a scene witnessed by a horrified William Rivers.

Nevertheless, frontline psychotherapy was being practised, as reported by Eugene Minkowski, a young military doctor who took part in the Battle of the Somme and the Battle of Verdun. Such therapy was also conducted between the men, in infirmaries, and with stretcher-bearers like my maternal grandfather. His war buddies told my father later that he would raise their morale with his music. His enigmatic explanation: "I was a stretcher-bearer because I was in the band" became clearer when I read the article by Irish military psychiatrist Morgan O'Connell, entitled "The Falkland Experience, 1982".[5]

Called up to fight in the Falklands War, O'Connell recounts his crossing of the Atlantic with the troops, without any staff to help the men deal with the fear of what awaited them. On the ship, he relied on military bands, whose members became stretcher-bearers during the conflict, "as is the custom in the British Army", and no doubt in the French Army as well.

To sing, or to write, be it in diaries in an Intensive Care Unit or in black moleskine notebooks brought back from the front, on scraps of paper and in letters exchanged with the home front, are practices going back through the history of wars all the way to Antiquity.

Notes

1 Barrois, C., *Les névroses traumatiques*, Paris: Dunod, 1988; *La psychanalyse du guerrier*, New York: Hachette, 1993.
2 My warm thanks to Emmanuel Saint-Fuscien for inviting us to speak, with Stéphane Tison.
3 Tison, H. and Guillemain, S., *Du front à l'asile, 1914–1918*, Paris: Alma Éditeur, 2013.
4 Barker, P., *The Regeneration Trilogy*, op. cit.
5 O'Connell, M., "The Falkland Experience, 1982", Royal Navy Hospital Hasplar, in *Combat Psychiatry*, March 1985.

Chapter 12

Writers as Valuable Travelling Companions

Homer and Virgil

In the early 2000s we met Jonathan Shay, author of *Achilles in Vietnam*[1] and psychiatrist at the Boston Veterans Hospital for Vietnam veterans with PTSD (Post-Traumatic Stress Disorder).

The acronym was created in 1980 and entered into the DSM-5 (Diagnostic and Statistical Manual of Mental Disorders) in order to justify paying pensions to veterans whose symptoms persist or get worse with age. Thomas Salmon was one of the first to recognise this problem, as well as the need for therapeutic and community centres for elderly veterans, where their experiences can be validated and no longer stigmatised. The veterans' tragic experiences can be glimpsed in old French traditional songs like "*Brave marin revient de guerre tout doux* (Brave sailor comes back from war, silently" (1792), in novels like Balzac's *Colonel Chabert*,[2] and in epic poems.

Jonathan Shay told us that thanks to his daughter who was a student at Harvard, he attended classes on the Trojan War given by Hellenist Gregory Nagy. She had told him: "He says the same things as you do". It happened that we had just met Gregory Nagy, who had come to speak at our seminar in 2002, at the invitation of our mutual friend, Hellenist Nicole Loraux.

During the seminar, Nagy had commented on a verse from Virgil's first book of the *Aeneid*.[3] After fleeing Troy with his companions and losing them during the crossing of the Mediterranean, Aeneas lands at Carthage with his *therapon* Achates, and weeps for the first time. While waiting for Queen Dido, he observes the temple built by the queen, discovers that the metopes carved in bas-relief tell the story of "his" war, and recognises himself on the frieze. The fact that strangers testify to his experience puts an end to his dissociation. The verse discussed by Nagy—that Victor Hugo would use as the title of one of his poems[4]—expresses succinctly, in rhythmic scansion, the sudden thawing of traumatic anaesthesia. This is Nagy's translation, quoted from memory:

Sunt lacrimae rerum, et mentem mortalia tangunt.

DOI: 10.4324/9781003257592-14

"There are tears in the universe and mortal things touch the mind".

This psychotherapeutic process touches the *men*—the mind, which makes it possible to learn—as Nagy emphasises. A connection is made with language, thought and the passage of time, thanks to "the relief"—in both senses of the term—of an alterity—the foreign queen—appearing on the two-dimensional, "filmy" world of trauma. The "witness to events without a witness" Dori Laub speaks about.[5] Even when these events are recorded in writing, they often remain without any witness, at the bottom of a drawer or in an attic, and only occasionally resurface after someone's death.

Historians restore their testimonial value by bringing them out of anonymity. Stephane Audoin-Rouzeau book *Quelle histoire*[6] is based on a few pages written by his grandfather, Robert Audoin, about a long night of terror, on August 25, 1916, "quickly recorded, as it was fated never be forgotten".

Les cicatrices rouges 14–18,—"Red Scars"[7] by Annette Becker, about the atrocities endured by civilian populations in the occupied territories of France and Belgium, is based on personal diaries, "often kept by women who perceived the depths of evil, experienced the suffering inflicted, and decided to take risks to bear witness to them".

Allons enfants de la patrie[8]—the first line of the anthem *La Marseillaise*—by Manon Pignot is a collection of letters written by children during the First Word War, and kept in schools or in families, such as Françoise Dolto's correspondence referred to earlier. In his little book *Salut Poilu*[9]—"poilu" was the name given to French soldiers in the First World War—Loïc Jaquet literally walks in the traces of his great uncle, a stretcher-bearer from Beaujolais, on the site of the battle of Crouy, using the information given in a letter written by the soldier to his wife in January 1915.

While I write this I ask myself whether the tears of Jessica's patient when he came out of the coma do not echo Virgil's verse. She said: "He realised that something very serious had happened to him". Mortal things could touch his mind, thanks to Jessica's presence.

When descendants of war veterans mention their writings, ignored for generations, I ask for them. One day, a young man handed me his great-grandfather's notebook, someone who must not have been highly regarded in the family, judging by his descendant's comment: "Look what the fool wrote". I read some passages aloud and saw the young man cry for the first time. Tears contained in mortal things touched his mind, which became able to learn. *Sunt lacrimae rerum.*

Achilles in Vietnam

What Jonathan Shay learned in Gregory Nagy's lectures led to the writing of *Achilles in Vietnam*, the book in which Shay defines trauma as betrayal by one's command. At the start of the Iliad[10]; on, Achilles' rage in his barracks resonates for Shay with the anger of the men he sees at the hospital. In the epic work, the "best of the Achaeans" remains furious and refuses to go back into battle after Agamemnon, the King of kings, breaks his word and takes the hero's war prize, Briseis, for himself. When Patroclus, Achilles' second in combat, decides to go back to fight wearing Achilles' armour and is killed by Hector, the hero is distraught by the death of his *therapon*. He is no longer himself.

"I died at Ypres, at Cambrai, at Amiens", Bion says, where the men in his tank crew were killed. My mother used to say that my grandfather's war buddy "meant more to him than his family".

The subtitle of *Achilles in Vietnam* is *Combat Trauma and the Undoing of Character*. After Patroclus' death, Achilles goes "berserk"—a word that comes from Old Norse meaning madly furious, out of control. This is how he appears to Hector, half god, half beast, terrifying the Trojan hero with his curses. True to his word, after killing him, he defiles his corpse by dragging it behind his chariot around Patoclus' tomb, and refuses to give it back to his father, King Priam, as the laws of war require.

According to Jonathan Shay, a similar rage seizes soldiers betrayed by civilians who treat them like murderers or nobodies. When young Bion was on home leave in London during the war, this attitude made him want "to desert towards the frontline", in order to be with his companions again. A similar loneliness experienced by children or adults seduced and abused by relatives, family friends, churchmen, teachers or caregivers provokes the same rage, often turned against oneself, to the point of suicide. Who can be trusted, who should they attack when they were betrayed in the name of love and humanity?

What can be trusted is the poet's rhythmic breath, which spans the centuries and reanimates us.

The breath of epics, of jazz and of laughter

When he heard the scansion of dactylic hexameters, Jonathan Shay was reminded of the veterans' expletives that he "tried to quote as exactly as possible: fucking colonel, fucking confused, fucking unit, fucking medals, mother fucker!", etc. He realised that the beat of such curses breathed life into zones of death. Using political satire with another scansion, André Chenier, imprisoned during Reign of Terror of the French Revolution, composed his *Iambes*,[11] that unleashed a paroxysm of violence, and smuggled them out of the Saint Lazare prison in a laundry basket in 1794, a few days before his execution.

In more recent times, the "beat" set the rhythm of Jack Kerouac's prose when he typed the manuscript of *On the Road*[12] in three weeks, on a single roll of paper, and when he recited it to improvised jazz played on the piano by Thelonius Monk, who was hearing it for the first time. This beat punctuates Kerouac's encounters with Americans strewn onto the roads by the post-war period. In 1949, when he reached San Francisco, this beat inspired the performance of a prodigious Afro American tenor saxophone player nicknamed *Blow man*, whose audience would shout: "Blow, man, blow!"

The poetic rhythm also offers a literary tomb to errand souls: to Kerouac's beloved older brother, Gerard, who died at the age of nine after a long illness, when Jack was four; and to Cervantes' companions in battle, killed at the Siege of La Goulette, for whom he wrote poems in the first *Don Quixote*. The only piece of music Maurice Ravel composed at the front—a tribute to his mother upon her death—was "Le Tombeau de Couperin".

The breath which thaws frozen emotions is also that of laughter, recommended to his readers by the eminent physician François Rabelais. Laughter breaks out in the hair parlour improvised at Jessica's initiative in her patient's room. It explodes when the respirator stops ringing after Emmannuelle promises a patient in an artificial coma to buy him a drink when he leaves the hospital, if he stops the noise! Such is the tone of Rabelais' address to the reader, which opens *Gargantua and His Son Pantagruel*[13]:

> Thinking therefore how sorrow might your mind Consume,
> I could no apter subject find;
> One inch of joy surmounts of a grief a span;
> Because to laugh is proper to the man.

However, Rabelais does not do away with grieving for the dead. In Chapters 55 and 56 of Book IV, frozen words fall onto the deck of Pantagruel's ship, "like sugar-plums of many colours". The captain informs him that they are the cries of men and women who died last winter in that place on the icy sea, in "a great bloody fight. Then the words [...] froze in the air", together with the neighing of horses, the sad cries of children, "and all other marshal din and noise".

When the giant warms up red frozen words in his hand—*les mots de gueule,* "gueule" meaning "mouth", as well as red in heraldic vocabulary, in this case a reference to slit throats—the battle has found a witness. But later, when Panurge, the giant's jester, wants to preserve some of the sugar-plums in oil, Pantagruel stops him, saying: "'Tis a folly to hoard up what we are never like to want".[14] Neither pantagruelism, nor quixoticism or shandyism wish to nurture a fascination with horror.

In *Don Quixote*, Salmon's principles are outlined in a comical tone, at the slow pace of Rocinante and the donkey, the vectors of transference that "combat melancholy", Cervantes says. In the novel, he creates the Proximity of the knight and Sancho, his *therapon;* the Immediacy is that of surviving images which provoke lighting-quick attacks; the Expectancy emerges in the talking cure unfolding between the two heroes, which engenders mad hope, personified by Dulcinea. She is the Lady of Thoughts in courtly love, created in 12th century by warrior poets. As I mentioned at the beginning of this book, this feminine agency enters the scene when the law of men breaks down, in order to restore thought in "another world", as Nanosy calls it, which people on the outside cannot imagine. She is the one addressed in letters to sweethearts, fiancées, wives or wartime godmothers, found in the pockets of soldiers carried away by stretcher-bearers.

Socrates in times of war and pandemics

The Lady of Socrates's thoughts is Diotima. In the *Symposium*,[15] he quotes her when his turn comes to speak in praise of love, *Eros*. He introduces her as a prophetess. She is the "stranger" who postponed the outbreak of the plague in Athens, which nevertheless killed Pericles when the epidemic raged in Attica, between 430 and 425 BC, according to Thucydides' account.[16]

Diotima's discourse springs forth in contrast with that of the other guests. The "medicine woman" on the front lines of the plague points out the lineage of Eros as the source of life. His father is *Poros,* the passage—transference between therapist and patient—and his mother is *Penia*, poverty—a lack of means, both material and symbolic.

Alcibiades confirms this definition when he arrives, completely drunk, at the end of the Symposium. They let him in on condition that he delivers a speech in praise of Socrates, with whom he is madly in love. The handsome young Athenian—who was a *strategos* in the Peloponnesian wars, where Socrates fought under his command as a *hoplite*, a citizen-soldier—starts by lamenting that his master has rejected his repeated attempts to draw him into close intimacy. Socrates doesn't sleep with his disciples.

Then, Alcibiades goes on to praise the philosopher's daring on the battle-field. From atop his horse, he saw Socrates' endurance as he fought, with his bare feet clad only in sandals, and he witnessed his exceptional bravery. He also saw him standing immobile for a whole the day and night, listening to his *Daemon*, who points out the right course of action in the face of mortal danger. For instance, it helps him to prevent his companions from running away after a defeat, since they would been hunted down like game. When Alcibiades was wounded, Socrates tended to him physically and psycholog-ically, taking care of his weapons as well.

In the *Theaetetus*,[17] Socrates analyses transference in the psychotherapy of trauma as follows:

"Primary elements, *prôta stoicheia aloga*, are irrational. Grasped only by the senses, they cannot be known. Still, their names can intertwine, for it is the intertwining of names that makes the whole *logos*: speech and reason". The possibility of intertwining depends on the presence of an other able to give a name, *logon didonai,* to sensorial impressions, and through this transference allow the birth of a "transitional subject of speech"—to quote Gaetano Benedetti, psychoanalyst of schizophrenia in Basel.

When the tool with the names is broken, in wartime and during pandemics, when all symbolic resources are lacking, the therapist's porosity makes it possible to intertwine irrational elements, *aloga*, recorded by the senses, so that *logos* can be created. Nanosy says: "I had the impression that I was suffocating with them". And she keeps logs to intertwine words with the impressions she receives from unconscious patients who hear her above the black hole of the coma.

Notes

1 Shay, J., *Achilles in Vietnam*, op. cit.
2 Balzac, Honoré de, *Colonel Chabert*, New York: New Directions, 1997.
3 Virgil, *The Aeneid of Virgil*, New York: Charles Scribner's Sons, 1952.
4 Hugo, V., Sunt Lacrimae rerum, in *Les Voix Intérieures et les Rayons et les Ombres*, New York: Hachette, 2012.
5 Laub, D., *Une clinique de l'extrême*, op. cit.
6 Audoin-Rouzeau, S., *Quelle histoire. Un récit de filiation*, Paris: Seuil, 2013.
7 Becker, A., *Les cicatrices rouges 14–18*, Paris: Fayard, 2010.
8 Pignot, M., *Allons enfants de la patrie*, op. cit.
9 Jaquet, L., *Salut Poilu*, Paris: Éditions du Chameau, 2019.
10 Homer, *The Iliad*, London: William Heinemann Ltd., 1924.
11 Chenier, A., *Iambes*, Gallimard, 1958; *Poems*, F. Scarfe (Ed.), Oxford: Blackwell, 1961.
12 Kerouac, J., *On the Road*, New York: Viking Press, 1957.
13 Rabelais, F., *Gargantua and Pantagruel*, London: Penguin Classics, 2006.
14 Rabelais, F., *Gargantua and Pantagruel*, op. cit., Book IV, Chapter 51.
15 Plato, *Symposium*, Scotts Valley, CA: Create Space, 2013.
16 My thanks to Alfred Gillham for acquainting me with David Jones's *In Parenthesis*, with a Preface by T. S. Eliot (Faber & Faber, 1978). In 1933, the Welsh poet recounted his war in the trenches, intertwining his story with Welsh epic tales and other literary works, and quoting Alcibiades' praise of Socrates, as we do here.
17 Plato, *Plato's Theaetetus*, New York: The Liberal Arts Press, 1955.

Conclusion

Just as I was finishing this book, Dame Fortune, so dear to Boccacio, led me to take part in a video conference organised in Mexico by Alberto Montoya,[1] on the theme "Transliteralities in the Time of the Pandemic".

The conference brought together artists in different fields: cinema, painting, poetry... with researchers in other fields: history, psychoanalysis and biology. The first speaker, Luis Arturo, specialist in Aztec mythology, showed us images of the healing of patients on the front lines of the 16th-century smallpox pandemic, which killed three quarters of the population of Mexico City.

The images were taken from the Florentine Codex,[2] a text translated from Nahuatl by the monk Bernardino Sahagun, describing the customs of the inhabitants of New Spain. The passage about the disease called "Cocolitzli" shows in pictographs—the glyphs of Aztec writing—the *curandero*'s transference with the bedridden patient whose skin is covered in red spots. A bubble projecting from the medicine man's mouth, Arturo points out, shows the crucial role of speech in the treatment, and also conveys "the beauty" of mythological tales told to the rhythm of chants and dances.

Certainly, beauty is a major element, often mentioned in testimonies. Franck said: "This collective dynamic was very beautiful. I would like it to continue". Indeed, the marvel of such encounters is often erased by the return to normal life. I transcribed their front lines testimonies in haste, as if they might soon be lost. Why did I have this feeling? A story of front-line treatment had remained sketchy in my memory for 72 years, and would never have been told if I had not questioned my father about it a short time before he died at the age of 103, asking: "How did it really happen?"

I had some scant elements of the story. It happened at the start of 1945. Some leaders of the Resistance in the Tarentaise Valley where I was born—now famous for its ski resorts—were gathered in our kitchen. We lived in a *fruitière*, a house where the "common fruit", the Beaufort cheese produced on the high pastures, matured in cellars that were also used to hide food and weapons during the war.

I was one and a half when it happened. I put my hands on the door of the blazing hot stove and then started to scream. Everyone ran off. Afterwards, I only knew that I had been treated by "the doctor of the Resistance", as if the Resistance had an official doctor. Seventy-two years later, this "primary irrational element" intertwined with the words of the story I was told at long last.

My father carried me, while I kept howling, into a pharmacy he knew to be trustworthy. We were taken to a back room, and a young man came in—the doctor mentioned earlier. "What did he look like? —Dressed like a bum, we didn't have anything then. He took you on his lap, you stopped screaming right away and you kept looking at him. He asked the pharmacist for ointment and bandages. You let him do what he was doing. He said you would heal without a trace. I wanted to pay him, but he refused. —What was his name? —I don't know. —You saw him again? —Never, he must have been shot like the others".

He was my first psychotherapist, I thought, visualising his words like those in the bubble of the Codex which has survived for centuries. With these words were probably intertwined many others I gathered amid transferences with the folly of wars and traumas, and recently on the front line of the pandemic.

Notes

1 Montoya, A., *Paisajes de la locura,* Mexico: Para Digina, 2006; *Acompanar la locura. En las encrucijadas de un Sancho Panza*, Mexico: Circulo psicoanalitico mexicano, 2017; *El psycoanalysta en el cine*, Mexico, 2019.
2 Florentine Codex, Book XII, 53. See also Johansson, P., *La Palabra de los Aztecas,* Mexico: Trillias, 1993.

Bibliography

A Beautiful Mind, film, R. Howard (Dir.), 2001, based on the novel by Sylvia Nasar, New York: Touchstone, 1998.

Anonymous, *The Song of Roland*, D. L. Sayers (Trans.), Penguin Books, 1957.

Arbousse-Bastide, P., Auguste Comte et la folie, in *Les sciences de la folie*, R. Bastide (Ed.), Paris: Mouton, 1972.

Arendt, H., Totalitarianism, in *The Origins of Totalitarianism*, Cleveland, OH: The World Publishing Company, 1951, p. 350.

Audoin-Rouzeau, S., Article "Nous ne reverrons jamais le monde que nous avons quitté il y a un mois (We will never go back to the world we left a month ago)", on Mediapart, April 12, 2020.

Audoin-Rouzeau, S., *Quelle histoire. Un récit de filiation*, Paris: Seuil, 2013.

Baillet, A. (1691). *La Vie de Monsieur Descartes*, Paris: La Table ronde, 1946.

Balzac, Honoré de, *Colonel Chabert*, New York: New Directions, 1997.

Barker, P., *The Regeneration Trilogy*, London: Penguin Books, 1992.

Barrois, C., *Les névroses traumatiques*, Paris: Dunod, 1988.

Barrois, C., *Psychanalyse du guerrier*, New York: Hachette, 1993.

Becker, A., *Les cicatrices rouges* 14–18, Paris: Fayard, 2010.

Becker, A., *Les Messagers du désastre. Raphael Lemkin, Jan Karski et les génocides*, Paris: Fayard, 2018.

Beers, C., *A Mind that Found Itself*, Pittsburgh, PA: Pittsburgh University Press, 1981.

Benedetti, G., *The Psychotherapy of Schizophrenia*, New York: New York University, 1987.

Binswanger, L. and Warburg, A., *La Guérison infinie*, D. Stimili (Ed.), Paris: Rivages, 2007.

Bion, W., *A Memoir of the Future*, London: Karnac, 1981.

Bion, W., *All My Sins Remembered*, London: Karnac, 1985.

Bion, W., *The Long Week-End*, London: Karnac, 1982.

Bion, W. R., *Brazilian Lectures*, London and New York: Routledge, 1990.

Bion, W. R., *Clinical Seminars and Other Works*, London: Karnac, 1987; Sao Paulo lectures, 1978.

Blank, A., Sonnenberg, S., and Talbott, J., *Stress Recovery in Vietnam Veterans*, Washington, DC: American Psychiatry Press, 1985.

Boccaccio, G., *The Decameron*, London: Penguin Classics, 2003.

Bond, E., *Thomas Salmon, Psychiatrist*, New York: Norton, 1950.

Caruth, C., *Listening to Trauma: Conversations with the Leaders in the Theory & Treatment of Catastrophic Experience*, Baltimore, MD: Johns Hopkins University Press, 2014.

Cervantes, M., *Don Quixote I*, The Author's Preface, Canterbury Classics, Charlotte, NC: Baker & Taylor, 2013.

Chenier, A., *Iambes*, Gallimard, 1958; *Poems*, F. Scarfe (Ed.), Oxford: Blackwell, 1961.

Chernow, W., *The Warburgs*, New York: Vintage Books, 1994.

Cooperman, M. (1970). Defeating Processes in Psychotherapy, in Transactions of the Topeka Psychoanalytic Society, *Bull. of the Menninger Clinic* 34: 36–38.

Davoine, F., *A Word to the Wise*, London: Routledge, 2018.

Davoine, F., *Fighting Melancholia*, London: Karnac, 2016.

Davoine, F., *Mother Folly: A Tale*, Stanford, CA: Stanford University Press, 2014.

Davoine, F., *Wittgenstein's Folly*, New York: YBK Publishers, 2012.

Davoine, F. and Gaudillière, J.-M., *History beyond Trauma*, New York: Other Press, 2004.

De Rotelande, H. (late 12th century), *Ipomedon*, Klincksieck, 1979.

Delaporte, S., and Salmon, T. W., *Le Médecin des "sans voix" et des soldats, pour une autre psychiatrie (1872–1927)*, forthcoming.

Descartes, R., Olympica, in *Vie de Monsieur Descartes*, op. cit.; *Discourse on Method and Meditations*, New York: Dover Philosophical Classics, 2003; *The Correspondence between Princess Elisabeth of Bohemia and René Descartes*, Chicago, IL: University of Chicago Press, 2007.

Dolto, F., *L'Image inconsciente du corps* (The Unconscious Image of the Body), Paris: Seuil, 1984.

Drury, M. O'C., Conversations with Wittgenstein, in *Ludwig Wittgenstein. Personal Recollections*, R. Rhees (Ed.), Oxford: Blackwell Publishing, 1981.

Elshtain, J. B., *The Jane Addams Reader*, New York: Basic Books, 2012.

Erasmus, D., *The Praise of Folly*, London: Aeterna Press, 2010.

Favrot Peterson, J. and Terraciano, K. (Eds.), *Florentine Codex*, Book XII, Austin: University of Texas Press, 2019.

Frazer, J. G., *The Golden Bough: A Study in Magic and Religion*, Oxford: Oxford Paperbacks, 2009.

Freud, A. and Dann, S. (1951). An Experiment in Group Upbringing, in *Psychoanalytic Study of the Child* 6: 127–168.

Freud, S., *A Project for a Scientific Psychology*, S.E. 1, London: Hogarth, pp. 281–397.

Freud, S., *Delusions and Dreams in Jensen's Gradiva*, S.E. 9, London: Hogarth, 1907.

Freud, S. (1916–1917). *Introduction to Psychoanalysis*, Chicago, IL: Independent Publishing, 2020.

Freud, S., *The Uncanny*, S.E. 17, London: Hogarth, 1919.

Freud, S. and Breuer, J., *Studies on Hysteria,* S.E. 2, London: Hogarth, 1895.

Fromm-Reichmann, F., *Principles of Intensive Psychotherapy*, Chicago , IL: University of Chicago Press, 1950.

Gaudillière, J.-M., *Madness and the Social Link. Seminars 1985–2000*; *The Birth of a Political Self* (Seminars 2001–2014), London: Routledge, 2020.

Gouhier, H., *La Vie d'Aguste Comte*, Paris: Vrin, 1997; Pickering, M., *Auguste Comte: An Intellectual Biography*, Cambridge: Cambridge University Press, 1993.

Greenberg, J., *I Never Promised You a Rose Garden*, New York: Signet, 1989.

Groddeck, G., *The Book of the It*, Eastford, CT: Martino Fine Books, 2015.

Haldane, E. S., *DESCARTES His Life and Times*, London: John Murray, 1905.

Hellzapoppin, film, Potter, H. C. (Dir), 1941.

Homer, *The Iliad*, London: William Heinemann Ltd., 1924.

Hornstein, G., *To Redeem One Person is to Redeem the World. The Life of Frieda Fromm-Reichmann*, New York: The Free Press, 2000.

Hugo, V., Sunt Lacrimae rerum, in *Les Voix Intérieures et les Rayons et les Ombres*, New York: Hachette, 2012.

Humbert, Capitaine, *La Division Barbot*, New York: Hachette, 1919.

Jaquet, L., *Salut Poilu*, Paris: Éditions du Chameau, 2019.

Jeux interdits, film, Clement, R. (Dir.), 1952.

Johansson, P., *La Palabra de los Aztecas,* Mexico: Trillias, 1993.

Jones, D., *In Parenthesis*, London: Faber & Faber, 1978; Preface by T. S. Eliot.

Kerouac, J., *On the Road*, New York: Viking Press, 1957.

Koerner, J. L., Writing Rituals: The Case of Aby Warburg, in *Common Knowledge* 18(1): 86–105, Duke University Press, 2012.

Kohut, H., *The Analysis of the Self. Psychoanalytic Treatment of Narcissistic Personality Disorders*, Chicago, IL: University of Chicago Press, 1971.

La Fontaine, J. (1678). The Animals Ill with the Plague, in *The Complete Fables of Jean de La Fontaine*, N. R. Shapiro (Trans.), Champaign: University of Illinois Press, 2007, p. 156.

Lacan, J., On a Question Preliminary to Any Possible Treatment of Psychosis, in *Écrits: A Selection*, A. Sheridan (Trans.), London: Tavistock/Routledge, 1977.

Lacan, J., Remarks on Psychic Causality, in Le *Problème de la psychogenèse des névroses et des psychoses*, H. Ey (Ed.), Paris: Desclée de Brouwer, 1950, and in *Écrits*, Paris: Seuil, 1966.

Lacan, J., *The Seminar of Jacques Lacan. Book VII. The Ethics of Psychoanalysis 1959–1960*, London: Routledge, 1992.

Lacaze, A., *The Tunnel*, B. W. Dower (Trans.), London: Penguin Books, 1978.

Landau, M. (1990). Les enfants de Terezin, in *Le temps du non: Psychanalyse et Idéologie* 5: 45–51.

Laub, D. (1937–2018). *Une clinique de l'extrême*, Le Coq-Héron, 2015, No. 220–221, érès; *Entretien avec Françoise Davoine* (interview), Le Coq-Héron, 2013, No. 214, p. 145.

Malpertu, Y., *Une liaison philosophique. Du thérapeutique entre Descartes et la princesse Elizabeth de Bohême*, Paris: Stock, 2012.

Masson, J. M. (Ed.), *The Complete Letters of Sigmund Freud to Wilhelm Fliess, 1887–1904*, Cambridge, MA: Harvard University Press, 1985.

Mohatt, G., and Eagle Elk, J., *The Price of a Gift. A Lakota Healer's Story*, Lincoln: Nebraska University Press, 2000.

Monk, R., *Ludwig Wittgenstein: The Duty of Genius*, London: Penguin Books, 1990.

Montoya, A., *Paisajes de la locura*, Mexico, Para Digina, 2006; *Acompanar la locura. En las encrucijadas de un Sancho Panza*, Mexico, Circulo psycoanalitico mexicano, 2017; *El psycoanalysta en el cine*, Mexico, 2019.

Moore, W., Schrödinger, *Life and Thought*, Cambridge: Cambridge University Press, 1989.

Morrison, T., *Beloved*, Richmond: Alma Classics, 2017.

Nasar, S., *A Beautiful Mind*, New York: Simon & Schuster, 1998.

O'Connell, M., "The Falkland Experience, 1982", Royal Navy Hospital Hasplar, in *Combat Psychiatry*, March 1985.

On Men and War, film, Bécue-Renard, L. (Dir.), 2014.

Owen, W. (1893–1918). *The War Poems*, London: Sinclair-Stevenson, 1994.

Paulhan, J., *L'expérience du proverbe*, Bordeaux: L'échoppe, 1993.

Perry, E. S., *Psychiatrist of America: The Life of Henry Stack Sullivan*, Cambridge, MA: Belknap Press, 1982.

Pignot, M., *Allons enfants de la patrie*, Paris: Seuil, 2012.

Plato, *Plato's Theaetetus*, New York: The Liberal Arts Press, 1955.

Plato, *Symposium*, Scotts Valley, CA: Create Space, 2013.

Rabelais, F., *Gargantua and Pantagruel*, London: Penguin Classics, 2006.

Rivers, Captain W., The Repression of War Experience, in *The Lancet*, February 2, 1918.

Ross, I. C., *Laurence Sterne, A Life*, Oxford: Oxford University Press, 2001.

Sassoon, S. (1886–1967). *The War Poems*, London: Faber & Faber, 2014.

Savall, J., *Don Quijote de la Mancha – Romances y Musicas*, CD, Alia Vox, Spain, 2006.

Scarlatti, A. (1721). *La Griselda*; Vivaldi, A. (1735). *Griselda*; Massenet, J. (1901). *Griselidis*.

Schields, C., *And So It Goes, Kurt Vonnegut, a Life*, New York: Henry Holt and Company, 2011.

Schrödinger, E., *What Is life? With Mind and Matter and Autobiographical Sketches*, Cambridge: Cambridge University Press, 2012.

Schur, M., *Freud: Living and Dying*, New York: International Universities Press, 1972.

Shakespeare, W., *Hamlet*, New York: Simon & Shuster, 2003. Act I, sc. 5, v. 189.

Shay, J., *Achilles in Vietnam*, New York: Scribner, 1995.

Shephard, B., *A War of Nerves. Soldiers and Psychiatrists in the Twentieth Century*, Cambridge, MA: Harvard University Press, 2003.

Sterne, L., *The Life and Opinions of Tristram Shandy, Gentleman*, London: Norton, 1980.

Sullivan, H. S., *Schizophrenia as a Human Process*, London: W.W. Norton, 1981; The *Fusion of Psychiatry and Social Sciences*, London: W.W. Norton, 1971.

Sullivan, H. S., Schizophrenic Individuals as a Source of Data for Personality Research, in *Schizophrenia as a Human Process*, London: W.W. Norton, 1974.

Thom, R., To *Predict Is Not to Explain*, Toronto: Thombooks Press, 2016.

Tison, H. and Guillemain, S., *Du front à l'asile, 1914–1918*, Paris: Alma Éditeur, 2013.

Tweedy, R. (Ed.), *The Political Self*, London: Karnac Books, 2017.

Van der Kolk, B., *The Body Keeps the Score*, New York: Penguin Books, 2014.

Virgil, *The Aeneid of Virgil*, New York: Charles Scribner's Sons, 1952.

Vonnegut, K., *Slaughterhouse-Five*, Piscataway, NJ: Research & Education Association, 1996.

Vonnegut, K., *Timequake*, New York: G. P. Putnam's Sons, 1997.

Wang, H., *Reflections on Kurt Gödel*, Cambridge, MA, and London: The MIT Press, 1987.

Warburg, A. (April 1939). A Lecture on Serpent Ritual, in *Journal of the Warburg Institute* 4: 277–292.

Wiginton, J., *Baba Yaga Tales*, Scotts Valley, CA: CreateSpace Publishing, 2018.

Winnicott, D. W. (1974). Fear of Breakdown, in *International Review of Psycho-Analysis* 1(1–2): 103–107.

Wittgenstein, L., *Philosophical Investigations*, G. E. M. Anscombe (Trans.), London: Basil Blackwell, 1958.

Wittgenstein, L. (1953). *Philosophical Investigations*, Oxford: Oxford University Press, 1983.

Wittgenstein, L., *Remarks on Frazer's Golden Bough*, in *Wittgenstein, Sources and Perspectives*, C. Grant Luckardt (author), Ithaca, NY: Cornell University Press, 1979.

Index

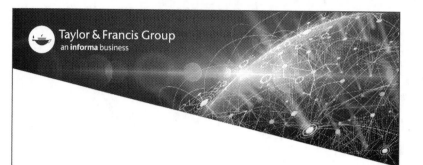

Printed in the United States
by Baker & Taylor Publisher Services